Wealth, Welfare and Sustainability

Wealth, Welfare and Sustainability

Advances in Measuring Sustainable Development

Kirk Hamilton

Lead Environmental Economist, Environmental Economics and Policy, The World Bank, Washington DC, USA

Giles Atkinson

Senior Lecturer in Environmental Policy, Department of Geography and Environment and Deputy Director, Centre for Environmental Policy and Governance, London School of Economics and Political Science, UK

Edward Elgar

Cheltenham, UK • Northampton, MA, USA

Published by
Edward Elgar Publishing Limited
Glensanda House
Montpellier Parade
Cheltenham
Glos GL50 1UA
UK

Edward Elgar Publishing, Inc.
136 West Street
Suite 202
Northampton
Massachusetts 01060
USA

A catalogue record for this book
is available from the British Library

ISBN-13: 978 1 84376 576 9 (cased)
ISBN-10: 1 84376 576 4 (cased)

Printed and bound in Great Britain by MPG Books Ltd, Bodmin, Cornwall

Contents

Figures

Tables

Preface and acknowledgements

This book is concerned with how current decisions about consumption and saving have an impact upon future well-being, and in particular how current measurable indicators can shed light upon the prospects for future well-being. It is concerned, in short, with the concept and measurement of sustainable development. This task is beset by conceptual and empirical challenges. Yet at the heart of this book lies a very practical concern – if sustainability is to mean anything at all it needs to be measurable. We feel a sense of urgency in this task. Because current systems of economic indicators do not clearly signal whether an economy is on a sustainable path, policy errors based on these indicators will continue to be made and perpetuated. Moreover, these errors have a long reach, since they affect not only current well-being but also the well-being of those living in the future. Our book builds upon a body of knowledge linking growth theory, asset accounting and indicators of sustainable development. Moreover, what we are particularly interested in is the empirical application of this accumulated knowledge.

We last approached the question of measuring sustainable development in Atkinson et al. (1997). With our co-authors in that volume we examined a broad array of proposals for the measurement of well-being and sustainability. The rationale for that approach was that a meaningful picture of whether countries are developing sustainably requires a judicious mix of indicators. Our aim in this current volume is more focused on the *economics* of sustainability and the role that saving in particular plays in determining whether economies are sustainable. There has been solid progress on this topic in the nearly 10 years since Atkinson et al. (1997), progress which merits a fresh look at the economic approach to measuring sustainable development.

This is a project that we began in the early 1990s with David Pearce. Sadly, David passed away suddenly in September 2005. Much has been and will be written elsewhere about David's immense contribution to the development of environmental economics as an academic discipline and a basis for policy. We heartily endorse all of these tributes. David was also famous for the generosity and encouragement that he showed to his many students and colleagues over the years, and we were certainly

xi

beneficiaries. We would like to add our own words of gratitude for David's major contribution to the work that is contained in this volume. David was struck by how the handful of green national accounting studies that had began to emerge in the late 1980s presented both a novel and ambiguous picture of development prospects. The picture was novel because new and exciting data were being presented about economic progress in the presence of resource depletion and environmental degradation. The ambiguity stemmed from the fact that these 'green GDP' estimates (as they became known) did not in practice provide a clear signal about whether development was sustainable or not. David's contribution, published originally in Pearce and Atkinson (1993), was a key insight: focus instead on net saving, the amount of saving over and above the value of *total* asset consumption. If the adjusted net saving rate was negative, it was argued, then this provides an indication that a country is eroding the capital on which its development depends. Much of the data used to add empirical substance to these claims was of a provenance that – at least from today's vantage point – could best be viewed as illustrative. Nor was the theory behind this claim fleshed out in anything more than a rudimentary way, although a handful of notable earlier contributions had certainly pointed in this practical direction. Yet, in setting out his intuitions, David put down an important marker for future work: improve the numbers, tidy up the theoretical details, and an insightful and practical indicator would result. While this original intuition proved correct, the literature of the last 10 years or so shows that 'filling in the details' has been a protracted process. We hope that ours is a useful contribution to this work in progress. We also hope very much that David would have approved of the extensions and refinements of his vision that we set out in this book.

We would like to thank the following people for valuable insights and inputs, particularly in chapters 4, 6, 7 and 9: Susana Ferreira, Giovanni Ruta, Liaila Tajibaeva, Walter Nalvarte and Katharine Bolt. We would also thank our many colleagues, including John Dixon, John Hartwick, John Proops and Jeffrey Vincent, who have been important sources of advice and support as we carried out this work.

KH
GA

1. Introduction

This book is concerned with how current decisions about consumption and saving have an impact upon future welfare, and in particular how current measurable indicators can shed light upon the prospects for future welfare. We are concerned both with the sustainability of development – with Pezzey (1989), we say that development is sustained along a development path if welfare does not decrease at any point along the path – and with development prospects as measured by the present value of welfare along a development path.[1] This places our emphasis squarely on wealth and what is happening to wealth, broadly construed, along any path.

The question of measurability is thus key. If current systems of economic indicators do not clearly signal that the economy is on an unsustainable path, then policy errors will be made and perpetuated. As will become clear below, this is more likely to be an issue for developing countries than developed, since these countries are more highly dependent on exhaustible resources as a share of economic activity. However, rapidly industrializing or developed economies – by degrading other environmental resources which might affect development prospects – are not immunized against these same questions.

The title of Weitzman's seminal paper on national income accounting – 'On the welfare significance of national product income in a dynamic economy' – neatly captures many of the key concerns of this book. Why, Weitzman asked, when one economic goal is to maximize consumption, do we measure income as the sum of consumption and investment? Weitzman's paper has spawned a very large literature, particularly with regard to the expansion of national income accounting to include a variety of natural assets. We will have occasion in this book to refer to much of this literature, but it suffices at this point to note that Hartwick (1990) and Mäler (1991) initiated the process of building the theoretical foundation for environmental accounting. Before that there was discussion of how a 'green' GNP (gross national product) could be measured and used, but little theoretical rigour was brought to bear on the problem (see, for example, Ahmad et al., 1989). So while these contributions presented a potentially novel and informative picture of development they raised as many (if not more) questions than they answered.

Pearce and Atkinson (1993) were among the first to posit a practical linkage between sustainable development and a measure of national wealth that was expanded to include natural resources. If sustainability is a matter of maintaining levels of welfare, then Pearce and Atkinson proposed that this was in turn a question of maintaining total wealth. They presented the first cross-country estimates of savings rates adjusted to reflect depletion and degradation of the environment. Subsequently Atkinson et al. (1997) and Hamilton and Clemens (1999) have updated both the theoretical argument,[2] linking savings and sustainability, and the empirical estimation of adjusted net savings rates – dubbed 'genuine' saving to distinguish it from traditional national accounting measures of net saving – for a wide range of countries. The World Bank has been publishing estimates of genuine saving as part of its *World Development Indicators* since 1999.

The key insight in the recent literature on an economic approach to national accounting is that future welfare is closely linked to current assets – or, to be more precise, to changes in real asset values. The notion of asset is quite broad, embracing produced capital, natural resources, human capital, knowledge, and pollution stocks (a type of negative asset or liability). A complete accounting must encompass all of these assets if consequences for future welfare are to be measured. This implies that measuring the sustainability of economies must go beyond simply 'greening' the accounts. It is important to note the deficiencies of standard national accounting in this context. The traditional measure of net saving, for example, simply deducts the depreciation of produced assets from gross saving. Since economies depend on a much wider array of assets for their development, this measure of net saving can say little about the changing asset base of the economy. This implies that traditional wealth and income measures are similarly incomplete.

This book is in many ways an extension of our work in Atkinson et al. (1997). But our aim in the current volume is more focused on the *economics* of sustainability and the role that the level of saving plays in determining whether economies are sustainable. The issues we will cover include population growth (existing assets have to be shared with more people), accounting for deforestation – forests are a multiple-use resource – and the effects of exogenous changes, both in technology and in resource prices. We also exploit the 30+ years of data on genuine saving to examine some important empirical issues: whether current saving actually measures changes in future welfare, savings and the resource curse (or 'paradox of plenty'), estimates of how rich economies would be if they had in fact invested resource rents over 30 years.[3] Finally we look at the pattern of international flows of resource rents in international trade using another model derived from the national accounts – Input/Output.

The individual chapters are introduced below. In each chapter we derive
the relevant theory and then develop an empirical application of it. For those
readers unfamiliar with the former, the resulting technical level may seem
demanding. However, rather than relegate these details on each occasion to
appendices, we feel that it is important to make it clear how practical, and
measurable, insights emerge from seemingly abtruse theory. To reverse the
logic, this also shows how empirical efforts to measure sustainability have
their justification in the theory of economic growth.

Chapter 2 lays out the basic theoretical framework for the book. It
develops a simple model with multiple assets and then derives the links
between sustainability, changes in social welfare and genuine saving. It then
derives a basic relationship between the change in current utility and the sign
and growth rate of genuine saving (see also Hamilton and Hartwick, 2005).
With the exception of the final empirical chapter on international flows of
resource rents, each chapter can be viewed as an extension or refinement
of the basic theoretical model. The general properties of genuine saving,
however, do not change as alternative models are developed.

Much of the work on greening the national accounts has dealt with
changes in total wealth – this is an important question, but it ignores the
impact of population growth on measures of total wealth per capita. If
population growth is an exogenous process[4] then we can informally express
the change in wealth K per capita N as,

$$\Delta\left(\frac{K}{N}\right) = \frac{K}{N}\left(\frac{\Delta K}{K} - \frac{\Delta N}{N}\right)$$
$$= \frac{\Delta K}{N} - \left(\frac{\Delta N}{N} \cdot \frac{K}{N}\right)$$

The first expression says that wealth per capita will be rising or falling
depending on whether the (percentage) growth rate of total capital is greater
or less than the population growth rate. This is nicely intuitive. The second
expression shows that the change in wealth per capita is also equal to saving
per person minus a 'Malthusian' term, the population growth rate times
the total wealth per capita. The Malthusian term represents the wealth-
diluting effect of population growth, whereby existing total assets have to
be shared with the population increment each year. Chapter 3 develops
the theory of asset accounting with exogenously growing population and
shows the considerable effect this has on the sustainability analysis of many
developing countries.

Turning from this measurement question, we proceed to a test of the
various measures of saving – gross, net, genuine, and genuine minus the

Malthusian term – to determine whether the historical data support the notion that current saving is equal to the change in future welfare, as theory would suggest. In Chapter 4 we develop a less restrictive model of saving and welfare change than the models employed in the literature. This leads to a testable hypothesis: does base year saving equal the present value of future changes in consumption?

Chapter 5 examines another important empirical question on savings and growth. There is a large and growing literature on the 'resource curse', also called the 'paradox of plenty'. Contrary to theory and intuition, resource-abundant countries have generally experienced lower growth rates in per capita gross domestic product or GDP than less resource-rich nations. We test two key propositions: (i) does low genuine saving contribute to low economic growth? and (ii) does the combination of high resource-dependence and negative genuine saving lead to particularly bad growth performance?

There is a close relationship between measuring sustainability and rules for sustainability. As noted above, the Hartwick Rule – invest resource rents – leads to constant welfare over time. This policy rule can equivalently be stated as 'set genuine saving equal to zero at each point in time', so that the indicator of sustainability, genuine saving, actually enters into the rule.[5] Chapter 6 develops an extension of the standard Hartwick Rule, to the effect that genuine saving should equal a positive constant value at each point in time, and shows that this rule leads to unbounded rising consumption in a simple exhaustible resource (Dasgupta–Heal) economy. We then proceed to examine the question 'How rich would countries be if they had followed the standard or extended Hartwick Rules for the past 30 years?' The results are, in many cases, striking.

Forests are a particularly complex resource to treat in accounting systems. However, in order to demonstrate the relevance of the basic framework used throughout this book, these complications merit attention here. The complexity itself is due in part to the multiple functions provided by forests – these resources provide timber and non-timber products, carbon sequestration, external benefits (water regulation and soil protection) and habitat for biodiversity. Moreover, some of these functions are valued by those living outside of countries with such forests, as well as those within the host country itself. Chapter 7 develops a model of deforestation at the frontier, where forested land is cleared, the timber burned, and the land is converted to agriculture. The model suggests how deforestation, entailing a change in multiple services from land, should be accounted for. This approach is applied to empirical data for the Peruvian Amazon.

An issue highlighted in the theoretical literature but not reflected in national accounting systems is the role of exogenous change in economic variables. An example of this would be an improvement in a country's terms of trade. If the improved terms of trade are permanent then the country is better off: it could consume more now without affecting its development prospects (the present value of future consumption). This is just another way of saying that the improved terms of trade should somehow be reflected in current measures of saving.

The next two chapters examine different aspects of exogenous change. Chapter 8 estimates the potential impact on savings and income of exogenous versus (costly) endogenous technological change in developed and developing countries. Chapter 9 measures 30-year natural resource price trends and estimates the impact on saving for natural resource exporters if these trends were to continue into the future.

Chapter 10 employs a different accounting framework, Input/Output accounting, in order to detail the inter-country flows of natural resource rents in international trade. The methodology accounts for both direct flows of rents, in the form of exports of resources, and indirect flows in the form of resources that are used to produce non-resource exports. The approach is applied to an empirical data set on international trade and resource rent generation to determine which countries are net exporters, and which net importers, of resource rents and to examine the dependence of economies such as the United States, the European Union and Japan on direct and indirect resource inputs from other countries. Finally, Chapter 11 sums up and offers some concluding remarks.

In this book we aim to reflect the progress that has been made in the literature on asset accounting since Atkinson et al. (1997). Understanding the centrality of net saving measures in assessing both the sustainability of development and the prospects for social welfare has been a major step forward in the theory of asset accounting. This provides a strong motivation for the chapters which follow dealing with *how* to measure net saving. But it also provides the basis for the empirical chapters which examine the links between savings and growth.

NOTES

1. We will use 'welfare' and 'utility' interchangeably in this introductory chapter.
2. Other key theoretical contributions include Dasgupta and Mäler (2000) and Asheim and Weitzman (2001).
3. The Hartwick Rule (Hartwick, 1977) states that economies can enjoy constant welfare, even in the face of essential exhaustible resources and fixed technology, as long as they invest resource rents in produced capital.
4. This means that population is growing independently (that is, outside the control) of other factors. We discuss the implications of relaxing this assumption in Chapter 3.
5. We note the point in Asheim et al. (2003) that current governments concerned with sustainability cannot commit future governments to behave sustainably, so that applying the Hartwick Rule *today* cannot ensure sustainability. But we would argue that the Hartwick Rule still has value as a prescription that, if followed at each point in time, will yield sustainability.

2. Wealth and social welfare

INTRODUCTION

This chapter will lay the basic theoretical foundation for much of the empirical work featured in the balance of the book. It proceeds from the consideration of measures of current utility to the problem of maximizing the present value of future utility. The properties of the constructs underlying this maximization problem provide the necessary framework for linking wealth, welfare and sustainable development.

If total wealth is related to social welfare, then changes in wealth should have implications for sustainability – this is the basic intuition of Pearce and Atkinson (1993). For optimal economies – economies where a planner can enforce the maximization of social welfare (that is, the maximization of the present value of utility) – a number of results have made the link explicit. Aronsson et al. (1997, equation 6.18) show that net saving in utility units is equal to the present value of changes in utility, using a time-varying pure rate of time preference. Hamilton and Clemens (1999) show that net or 'genuine' saving adjusted for resource depletion, stock pollutant damages and human capital accumulation is equal to the change in social welfare measured in dollars. They also establish that negative genuine saving implies that future utility must be less than current utility over some interval of time.

These results depend on the assumption that governments maximize social welfare. Dasgupta and Mäler (2000) show that net investment is equal to the change in social welfare in a non-optimizing framework where a resource allocation mechanism is used to specify the mapping from initial capital stocks to future stocks and flows in the economy. This result depends on accounting prices for assets being defined as the marginal changes in social welfare resulting from an increment in each asset (that is, accounting prices are the partial derivatives of the social welfare function). Arrow et al. (2003a) explore the accounting issues under a variety of resource allocation mechanisms.

The result linking net saving to changes in social welfare in Aronsson et al. (1997) can be extended to show that current saving equals the present value of changes in consumption in an optimizing economy. Dasgupta (2001) shows that the same is true in non-optimal economies where accounting prices are defined as above. Hamilton and Hartwick (2005) show that this relationship holds in an optimal economy, but their proof clearly only requires that the economy be competitive. This relationship between current saving and the present value of future changes in consumption is exploited in an empirical test of genuine saving in Chapter 4.

These main results on net saving and social welfare are derived below for a general multi-asset optimizing model.

In most of this book we assume that there is a fixed population. This permits us to focus on the pure asset accounting aspects of the problem, rather than the interaction between changes in assets and population growth. If population grows over time, as in virtually all developing countries, then changes in total wealth should take into account the change in population. Dasgupta (2001) shows that wealth per capita is the correct measure of social welfare if certain conditions are met: (i) population grows at a constant rate; (ii) per capita consumption is independent of population size; and (iii) production exhibits constant returns to scale. This book calculates wealth per capita as the measure of social well-being under these assumptions, as do Arrow et al. (2004). The measure of the change in wealth per capita derived in Chapter 3 below includes a specific adjustment for the immiserating effects of population growth. Arrow et al. (2003b) identify the correct welfare index in more general situations.

MAXIMIZING WELFARE OVER TIME

For a fixed population we will be concerned with maximizing the welfare of the 'representative individual'. This individual's utility function is assumed to embrace both consumption C and the levels of a series of N assets such as knowledge, healthfulness and natural and environmental resources. These assets are denoted as X_i and the utility function as $U(C, X_i)$. Assets can be 'bads', such as a stock of carbon dioxide, as well as goods such as a pristine natural area or commercial resources such as stocks of timber and minerals. While it is unlikely that individual welfare would depend directly upon the size of a reserve of oil in the ground or the stock of produced assets, it is convenient to define the problem in this very general way, since particular issues can easily be defined as special cases of the general problem.

Production proceeds via a production function $F(K, X_i, \dot{X}_i)$ which yields output of a homogeneous good which may be consumed, invested in produced capital K, or spent in amounts e_i for the control of the levels of the different stocks. That is, we assume control functions f^i such that $\dot{X}_i = f^i(X_i, e_i)$.

Util-denominated social welfare V is defined to be the present value of future utility, so that $V = \int_t^\infty U(C(s), X_i(s))e^{-\rho(s-t)}ds$. The pure rate of time preference ρ is fixed, while all other variables are assumed to be functions of time t, unless explicitly subscripted otherwise. This gives rise immediately to the following relationship:

$$U + \dot{V} = \rho V. \tag{2.1}$$

This expression hints at the linkage to national income accounting, since it states that utility plus the change in welfare is just equal to the 'return' on welfare.

The economic problem for this simple economy is to maximize the present value of future utility, that is, to maximize util-denominated welfare. This can be stated formally as follows:

$$\text{Max } V = \int_t^\infty U\big(C(s), X_i(s)\big)e^{-\rho(s-t)}ds \text{ subject to:}$$
$$\dot{K} = F - C - \sum e_i$$
$$\dot{X}_i = f^i(X_i, e_i).$$

THE HAMILTONIAN FUNCTION AND GENUINE SAVING

Solving this optimal control problem requires application of the Maximum Principle, which implies, among other things, that in order to maximize util-denominated welfare it is necessary to maximize the current value Hamiltonian function H at each point in time. For shadow prices γ_i this function is defined as follows:

$$H = U + \sum \gamma_i \dot{X}_i.$$

Note that for notational convenience we are assuming that $X_0 \equiv K$ – the stock of produced capital is not assumed to enter into the utility function, however. The shadow prices γ_i are defined in utils, with $\gamma_0 = U_C$ (the marginal utility of consumption). Shadow prices in consumption units can be derived by dividing these prices by the marginal utility of consumption:

$$p_i = \frac{\gamma_i}{U_C}.$$

Now it is possible to define genuine saving G precisely: it is equal to net investment[1] valued at shadow prices, so that,

$$G = \sum_i p_i \dot{X}_i. \qquad (2.2)$$

From this it follows immediately that,

$$H = U + U_c G. \qquad (2.3)$$

The Hamiltonian may be described as the utility prospect for the economy, since it combines both current utility and the contributions to future utility from current investment.

KEY RESULTS CONCERNING SAVINGS, WELFARE AND SUSTAINABILITY

The fundamental link between the Hamiltonian function and util-denominated welfare is derived in Appendix 2A.1. There it is shown that,

$$H = \rho V, \qquad (2.4)$$

expressions (2.1), (2.3) and (2.4) together imply that,

$$U_c G = \dot{V}. \qquad (2.5)$$

Genuine saving is equal to the change in social welfare divided by the marginal utility of consumption.

The third principal result on welfare and saving is also derived in the Appendix, where it is demonstrated that,

$$\dot{U} = U_c G \left(F_K - \frac{\dot{G}}{G} \right). \qquad (2.6)$$

Here F_K is the interest rate for the economy. By rearranging terms and expanding the expression for the change in utility, this yields

$$\dot{C} + \sum_i \frac{U_{X_i}}{U_C} \dot{X}_i + \dot{G} = F_K G. \qquad (2.7)$$

This is more intuitive: it says that the return on genuine saving equals the growth in saving plus the growth in a generalized measure of consumption at constant prices. This is a key link between growth and savings.

Expression (2.6) can also be solved as a differential equation, with particular solution,

$$G = \int_t^\infty \dot{U}(s) \Big/ U_C(s) \cdot \exp\left(-\int_t^s F_K(\tau)\,d\tau\right) ds. \qquad (2.8)$$

So genuine saving is equal to the present value of the change in utility, measured in dollars, along the optimal path.

PROPOSITIONS CONCERNING WEALTH, WELFARE AND SUSTAINABILITY

These results lay the cornerstone for four propositions linking current measures of utility, wealth defined as the present value of future utility, and the genuine saving rate. These propositions underpin much of the material in this book.

Proposition 2.1:   An optimal development path where genuine saving is always positive is a path where the present value of utility is always increasing (Dasgupta and Mäler 2000).

This follows immediately from expression (2.5). An increasing present value of utility is not precisely the same thing as sustainable development. But this proposition provides a powerful policy rule for decision-makers concerned with social welfare now and in the future.

Proposition 2.2:   If genuine saving is negative at a point in time on the optimal path, then utility at some point in the future must be less than current utility – that is, the path is unsustainable (Hamilton and Clemens 1999).

This follows from expressions (2.1) and (2.5): the present value of future utility can only be less than current utility if future utility is less than current utility over some interval of time. For decision-makers concerned with the sustainability of their economy, this provides a forward-looking indicator of unsustainability.

Proposition 2.3:   If genuine saving is always positive and growing at a percentage rate less or equal to the interest rate along a development path, then this path is sustainable and both current utility and the present value of utility are increasing everywhere along it.

Expression (2.6) provides the proof directly, a result first derived in Hamilton and Hartwick (2005). Hamilton and Withagen (forthcoming) show that this result holds in efficient competitive economies, where producers maximize profits, consumers maximize welfare, and governments internalize externalities through Pigouvian taxes – this raises the possibility of a general policy rule for sustainability.

Proposition 2.4: If the path of utility rises and then falls asymptotically to 0 with a single peak along the optimal development path, then genuine saving will turn negative prior to the peak.

This follows directly from expression (2.8). The result generalizes a proposition in Hamilton and Hartwick (2005), who derive the result for a Dasgupta–Heal economy where consumption does typically rise and then fall to 0 along the optimal path.

This proposition shows that negative genuine saving can be an 'early warning' for a myopic policymaker who does not know that the optimal development path is not, in fact, sustainable.

Definition 1: Consumption plus genuine saving equals narrow Hicksian income. This is a natural extension of the traditional definition of Hicksian income measured ex post: consumption plus change in assets. It is a narrow or limited measure because it includes only consumption of produced goods. The normative implications of measuring Hicksian income follow from Proposition 2.2: if a country's consumption of produced output exceeds its Hicksian income, then its genuine saving rate is negative and the optimal path is not a sustainable one.

CONCLUSIONS

These results indicate that there is an intrinsic relationship between changes in the value of assets, changes in social welfare along a development path and the sustainability of this path. For decision-makers concerned with social welfare, present and future, this places net investment in a wide range of assets at the heart of the policy issues concerning economic development.

An important point in all of this concerns welfare measurement or, to be more precise, the fact that direct welfare measurement is not required to guide development policy. The four key propositions hold for any specification of the utility function. The underlying theory tells us that measures of net investment or genuine saving for a sufficiently broad array of assets are sufficient to guide policy and to determine the direction of change of social welfare. As the balance of this book will show, the measurement issues for asset accounting are substantial. But succeeding chapters will also show that great progress has been made in techniques for asset accounting for a wide range of assets.

NOTE

1. This simple economy is closed to foreign trade, so that savings necessarily equal investment.

APPENDIX 2A.1: PROOF OF KEY RESULTS

The optimal path given (K_0, X_{i0}, ρ) is defined by the following problem (all variables are assumed to be functions of time and defined at time t unless explicitly denoted by a time subscript):

$$\text{Max } W = \int_t^\infty U\big(C(s), X_i(s)\big) e^{-\rho(s-t)} ds \text{ subject to:}$$
$$\dot{K} = F - C - \sum e_i$$
$$\dot{X}_i = f^i(X_i, e_i).$$

The current value Hamiltonian for this problem is $H = U + \Sigma \gamma_i \dot{X}_i = U + U_C G$, where G is genuine saving. Shadow prices are defined such that $\gamma_i = U_C p_i$ and are governed by the usual first order conditions:

$$\dot{\gamma}_i = \rho \gamma_i - \frac{\partial H}{\partial X_i}. \tag{2A.1}$$

In particular,

$$\frac{\dot{U}_C}{U_C} = \rho - F_K. \tag{2A.2}$$

The first order conditions,

$$\frac{\partial H}{\partial C} = \frac{\partial H}{\partial e_i} = 0 \tag{2A.3}$$

ensure that the path is optimal and that the Hamiltonian is maximized.

The principal results for this model can now be defined. First, note that for $H = H(C, e_i, X_i, \gamma_i)$,

$$\dot{H} = \frac{\partial H}{\partial C} \dot{C} + \sum \frac{\partial H}{\partial e_i} \dot{e}_i + \sum \frac{\partial H}{\partial X_i} \dot{X}_i + \sum \frac{\partial H}{\partial \gamma_i} \dot{\gamma}_i$$
$$= \sum \left(\frac{\partial H}{\partial X_i} + \dot{\gamma}_i \right) \dot{X}_i$$
$$= \rho \sum \gamma_i \dot{X}_i$$
$$= \rho U_C G.$$

This follows from expressions (2A.1) and (2A.3) and the fact that all variables are autonomous. This in turn implies that the present value Hamilton H^p has rate of change, $\dot{H}^p = -\rho e^{-\rho t} U$, and integrating forward gives, up to a constant of integration,

$$H^p = \rho \int_t^\infty U\big(C(s), X_i(s)\big) e^{-\rho s}\, ds + \lim_{s \to \infty} H^p(s).$$

The latter limit is assumed to be zero, a standard transversality condition for the growth problem. From this it follows that,

$$H = \rho V. \tag{2A.4}$$

It follows immediately from the definition of V that,

$$U + \dot{V} = \rho V,$$

which combined with expression (2A.4) and the definition of the Hamiltonian implies that,

$$\dot{V} = U_C G. \tag{2A.5}$$

The application of expression (2A.2) leads to the following result:

$$\dot{H} = \dot{U} + \dot{U}_C G + U_C \dot{G}$$
$$= \dot{U} + U_C \left(\frac{\dot{U}_C}{U_C} G + \dot{G} \right)$$
$$= \rho U_C G + \dot{U} - U_C \big(F_K G - \dot{G} \big).$$

From expressions (2A.4) and (2A.5) it can therefore be concluded that,

$$\dot{U} = U_C G \left(F_K - \frac{\dot{G}}{G} \right).$$

Finally, dividing this expression by U_C and expanding and rearranging terms yields,

$$\dot{C} + \sum \frac{U_{X_i}}{U_C} \dot{X}_i + \dot{G} = F_K G.$$

3.   Population growth and sustainability

INTRODUCTION

The *World Development Indicators* (World Bank, 2001) has highlighted since 1999 the 'genuine' rate of saving for over 100 countries around the globe. As a more inclusive measure of net saving effort, one that includes depletion and degradation of the environment, depreciation of produced assets and investments in human capital, genuine saving provides a useful indicator of sustainable development – the basic theoretical underpinnings of saving and sustainability were presented in Chapter 2. In the real world these theoretical results imply the common-sense notion that sustained negative rates of genuine saving must lead, eventually, to declining welfare.

An important point in all of this, of course, is that it is *per capita* welfare that must be sustained. Genuine saving measures the change in total assets rather than the change in assets per capita. While genuine saving is answering an important question, therefore – did total wealth rise or fall over the accounting period? – it does not speak directly to the question of the sustainability of economies when there is a growing population.[1] If genuine saving is negative then it is clear in both total and per capita terms that wealth is declining. For a range of countries, however, it is possible that genuine saving in total could be positive while wealth per capita is declining.

The practical difficulty in dealing with these questions is that there are no widely available statistics on total wealth. Many (but not all) OECD countries publish national balance sheet accounts, which measure the total value of produced assets and commercial land. Virtually no developing countries publish these accounts. Moreover, to be useful as a sustainability indicator, the total wealth figures must be very broad, encompassing produced assets, commercial land, natural resources, and human and social capital. In *Expanding the Measure of Wealth* (World Bank, 1997; see Kunte et al., 1998 for details) such a broad wealth measure was estimated for roughly 100 countries for 1994.[2]

This chapter will develop an approach to total wealth estimation, with the goal of estimating changes in wealth per capita. This approach refines the methodology of Hamilton (2003) by removing a significant downward bias

in the estimates of change in wealth per capita.[3] We report new estimates
of the composition of tangible wealth, showing that natural resources are
an important share of wealth in many developing countries. The analysis
proceeds by presenting a formal model of saving with a growing population,
followed by a detailed exposition of methodology for measuring changes
in wealth per capita, followed by a presentation of results for nearly 90
countries.

A FORMAL MODEL OF PER CAPITA SAVING

We assume that population N (equal to the labour force) growing at constant
rate g employs a constant returns to scale production technology $F = F(K, R,$
$A, N)$ to produce a homogeneous good which can be consumed or invested
in produced or human capital. Here K is produced capital, R is flows of an
exhaustible resource, and A is the stock of human capital – the stock of
knowledge and skills A is considered to be a factor of production distinct
from raw labour N. In per capita terms this becomes:

$$f = F/N = f(k,q,a,1), \text{ where } k = K/N, \text{ and } a = A/N.$$

For per capita consumption c, per capita utility $u(c)$, per capita education
expenditures e, per capita resource stock s, pure rate of time preference ρ,
and constant capital depreciation rate δ, a social planner aims to maximize
per capita welfare v as follows:

$$\max v = \int_t^\infty u\big(c(s)\big)e^{-\rho(s-t)}ds \text{ subject to:}$$
$$\dot{k} = f - c - e - \delta k - gk$$
$$\dot{s} = -q - gs$$
$$\dot{a} = w(e) - ga \tag{3.1}$$

Here $w(e)$ is the education (human capital investment) function and g is the
(constant) population growth rate.

　　Appendix 3A.1 below shows that total net or 'genuine' saving for this
model with growing population is given by

$$G_N = \big(n - F_R q + mw\big) - g\big(k + F_R s + ma\big), \tag{3.2}$$

where: $n = f - c - e - \delta k$ = net investment per capita in produced capital and m is the marginal cost of creating a unit of human capital.

Expression (3.2) therefore says that genuine saving is equal to net saving per capita minus a Malthusian term, the population growth rate times the total stock of wealth per capita. The intuition behind this is clear – wealth is built up as a result of saving effort, and is diminished to the extent that total wealth must be shared with each new population cohort.

The link between saving and welfare is also derived in Appendix 3A.1, where it is shown that,

$$u_c G_N = \dot{v}. \tag{3.3}$$

Expression (3.3) is the key welfare result concerning genuine saving. It states that genuine saving, measured in per capita terms,[4] is equal to the current change in per capita welfare (present value of utility) for the economy. For a social planner aiming to increase welfare, therefore, genuine saving is a key current indicator. Moreover, it follows from expression (3.3) that if genuine saving is negative at a point in time, then future utility must be less than current utility over some interval of time – negative genuine saving is therefore an indicator of unsustainability.

Expression (3.2) makes it clear that countries with high population growth rates are on a treadmill. Unless it is the case that the percentage change in total wealth is greater than the population growth rate, total wealth per capita will decline with consequences for future welfare.

These two expressions generalize in obvious ways when there are other arguments in the utility function and other assets in the economy. The estimation of genuine saving breaks down into two distinct pieces: calculating net saving per capita and calculating total wealth per capita. We now turn to the latter problem.

WEALTH ESTIMATION METHODOLOGY

Wealth is calculated below in a manner similar to that employed in Kunte et al. (1998), with some simplifications necessitated by data availability. For each country the basic procedure is to build asset accounts for each of the key categories of wealth for 1999. The steps are as follows.

Physical capital The stock of physical capital is calculated using a 'perpetual inventory model':

$$K_t = \sum_{i=t-n}^{t} I_i (1-\alpha)^i,$$ (3.4)

where the stock value is K, I is the value of investment in constant prices, and α is the depreciation rate. The accumulation period n is chosen to be 20 years (since structures make up typically 70 per cent or more of investment value and have relatively long service lives), while the rate of depreciation is 5 per cent (again reflecting the mix of relatively long-lived structures and short-lived machinery and equipment). This gives asset to GDP ratios of about 2 for rich countries, which matches what can be observed in the balance sheet accounts of countries such as Canada.

Agriculture, forestry and fisheries   Asset values for these renewable or provisionally non-depletable resources are derived from published data on valued added in the agriculture, forestry and fishery sectors. These sectors are typically lumped together in national accounts data as published in World Bank (2001). The combination of land rents, forest stumpage and fish resource rents is estimated to be 45 per cent of value added in the aggregate sector, based on figures reported in Kunte et al. (1998). It is assumed that these rents can be obtained in perpetuity, so that asset values are derived as the present value of an infinite rental stream, discounted at 4 per cent – the latter is a reasonable estimate of a 'world consumption rate of interest'.

Urban land   This is valued as a fixed proportion of the value of physical capital, since the majority of structures are on urban land. A value of 24 per cent of physical capital is used, again drawing on Kunte et al. (1998).

Mineral and energy wealth   Stocks of subsoil resources are valued according to the formula,

$$M_i = \left(p_i - c_i' \right) S_i,$$ (3.5)

for each resource i, where prices are world prices and c' is the marginal cost of extraction. The minerals and fuels covered include oil, natural gas, coal, bauxite, copper, gold, iron, lead, nickel, phosphate, silver, tin and zinc. Country-specific average cost data are derived as described in Hamilton and Clemens (1999). Marginal costs are assumed to be 15 per cent higher than average costs for all subsoil resources. Stock sizes (proven reserves) are capped at 20 times current production.

Discussion

The perpetual inventory method employed to estimate physical capital stocks is virtually the same as that employed in statistical offices around the world. A key difference, however, is that these agencies can differentiate between structures and machinery and equipment, and so can attain greater accuracy in stock estimates. For developing countries there are the additional complications that many investments, particularly in the public sector, do not pay off, and that rates of depreciation may be very high owing to lack of maintenance and spare parts. Physical capital estimates may therefore be biased upward in developing countries.

The assumption of perpetual resource rents in the agriculture, forestry and fishery sectors is optimistic in some cases, since it is precisely the unsustainable use of many of these resources that is placing development prospects at risk.

The mineral and energy wealth estimates are disputable in two regards. The assumed ratio of marginal to average costs is derived from Vincent (1997), who reports estimates for oil production in Malaysia, but generally speaking there are very few cost data available to permit derivation of more precise marginal cost figures. Secondly, proven reserves estimates for many minerals and energy types run to several decades or even centuries for some materials in some countries. Capping the reserve to production ratio at 20 is an explicitly conservative step, but consonant with a high degree of uncertainty concerning the value of many subsoil resources beyond a couple of decades.

It is certainly arguable that the value of external debt should figure in wealth estimation. These debts represent at least in part a claim on the returns to the total assets of indebted countries. However, examination of debt statistics (World Bank, 2001) reveals external debt to GNI ratios in excess of 80 per cent in nearly 40 countries – it is simply unclear whether these debts will ever be repaid, and they are not factored into the analysis of this chapter.

Selected Estimates of Wealth

Table 3.1 presents estimates of wealth for selected countries in Latin America, based on the preceding methodology and using data published in the *World Development Indicators* (World Bank, 2001).

This table reveals considerable variation in both levels and composition of wealth. It is apparent that minerals and energy are important sources of wealth in many countries in the region, even under the conservative assumptions adopted.

Table 3.1 Composition of wealth, selected countries, 1999

	Physical capital (%)	Agriculture, forest, fish (%)	Urban land (%)	Mineral wealth (%)	Energy wealth (%)	Wealth, per capita $	Wealth/ GNI
Argentina	63.7	19.7	15.1	0.2	1.3	22711	3.0
Bolivia	37.5	49.5	8.9	1.9	2.1	4486	4.5
Brazil	55.4	22.7	13.2	4.0	4.8	12619	4.2
Chile	49.3	21.7	11.7	17.1	0.2	16774	3.8
Colombia	45.2	34.0	10.7	0.1	9.9	9265	4.7
Costa Rica	48.1	40.4	11.4	0.0	0.0	13696	3.7
Ecuador	38.0	26.1	9.0	0.0	26.8	8395	6.1
El Salvador	45.4	43.8	10.8	0.0	0.0	6612	3.3
Guatemala	32.2	57.9	7.6	0.0	2.3	7360	4.5
Honduras	51.3	36.3	12.2	0.1	0.0	4398	5.2
Mexico	58.6	11.3	13.9	0.1	16.1	22055	4.6
Nicaragua	38.3	52.5	9.1	0.0	0.0	3284	8.3
Paraguay	40.8	49.5	9.7	0.0	0.0	8680	6.0
Peru	56.3	26.0	13.4	3.0	1.3	7753	3.9
Uruguay	54.0	33.2	12.8	0.0	0.0	16145	2.6
Venezuela	33.3	9.3	7.9	0.5	49.0	28320	6.6

If there is a clear outlier in this table it is Nicaragua, with total wealth eight times GNI. This may reflect the point mentioned in the discussion above, that in some developing countries the effectiveness of investment is extremely low – this would tend to overstate the values of physical capital in the table. The effectiveness of the use of assets may also be extremely low, which would inflate the wealth to GNI ratio.

MEASURING TOTAL GENUINE SAVING

The measure of total genuine saving employed in this chapter is largely similar to that reported in Hamilton and Clemens (1999) and published in World Bank (2001). There are a few methodological differences to be noted however.

Consumption of fixed capital   Hamilton and Clemens (1999) and World Bank (2001) use reported values of depreciation as published by the United Nations. To make the savings and wealth estimates consistent in the current exercise, expression (3.4) is used to derive depreciation estimates as follows:

$$CFC_t = K_t - K_{t-1} - I_t.$$

For high income countries this gives values (as a share of GDP) that are comparable with the United Nations figures. For low income countries there is in some cases considerable variance, owing, as noted in the section on wealth estimation, to the exaggerated levels of physical capital produced by the perpetual inventory model of asset accumulation.

Human capital   As in World Bank (2001), current education expenditures are treated as investment in human capital. However, it must be noted that this may overestimate the value of the investment in many low income countries – the government of Uganda, for example, recently estimated that only 16 cents on the dollar of public expenditure on education actually was making it to the village school. Lack of books and qualified teachers, and low completion rates for primary education, also make education expenditures relatively ineffective in poor countries. As in World Bank (2001), human capital is not depreciated.

Health capital   Certain expenditures on health (reproductive health, post-natal care, vaccinations and so on) can be considered to be investments to the extent that they create permanent increases in healthfulness, rather than providing pure consumption benefits or maintaining a given level of health. Grossman (1972) makes the point that investment in healthfulness creates an asset, a portion of human capital, that adds to both expected wages and to the enjoyment of illness-free time for other valued pursuits. Gates (1984) attempts to measure investment in health capital for the United States. Rich countries spend thousands of dollars per capita each year on health care (roughly $4300 in the USA in the late 1990s, for example). Much of this expenditure is either repair or consumption, rather than investment in healthfulness. It is assumed, therefore, that only expenditures up to $250 per capita represent investment (this is roughly the level of expenditure in upper middle-income countries) and expenditures per capita are capped at this level in the saving estimates.

Depletion of minerals and energy   To make the depletion estimates consistent with the wealth estimates (and consistent with the theoretical model), for physical quantity of extraction R the individual depletion values are derived as,

$$Depl_i = \left(p_i - c_i' \right) R_i.$$

The assumptions made about prices and marginal costs are identical to those in the wealth estimation.

Net forest depletion   As in Hamilton and Clemens (1999) and World Bank (2001), forest depletion is calculated as the difference between the rental value of growth and harvest. If there is net positive growth this is not included as an addition to saving, since it is likely that the trees in question (given the countries where this occurs) do not have commercial value.

Discussion

The saving estimates share the limitations of the figures published in World Bank (2001) in terms of coverage. In particular soil degradation and depletion of diamonds, subsoil water and fish are missing from the analysis, owing to limitations in the data sources. Deforestation (the change in land asset value when trees are cleared, including external and non-timber benefits of standing forest) is captured only imperfectly in the calculation of net forest depletion.

There are potential issues concerning the treatment of health and human capital in the saving estimates. In this analysis investments in health and human capital are treated as additions to saving, basically by reclassifying certain elements of consumption in the standard national accounts.

However, there is no corresponding asset in the wealth estimates, owing to genuine uncertainties in the methodology for accounting for these assets. This omission biases the net saving per capita estimates upward. Moreover, some education expenditures are arguably consumption (some students enjoy studying, at least some of the time), while, owing to data limitations, there is no estimate of depreciation of human capital – the effect of these omissions is also to bias the net saving per capita estimates upward.

Selected Results for Genuine Saving

Table 3.2 displays the components of genuine saving for selected Latin American economies as shares of GNI. As with the wealth estimates, these figures display a substantial degree of variation across the selected countries. The highest saver, Honduras, presumably benefited from aid inflows to finance repairs after Hurricane Mitch. The two countries with the heaviest dependence on oil extraction, Ecuador and Venezuela, both exhibit negative savings. Investments in healthfulness are very high, perhaps anomalously so, in Colombia and Nicaragua.

ESTIMATED CHANGES IN WEALTH PER CAPITA

Table 3A.1 at the end of the chapter presents the results of the calculation of changes in wealth per capita for nearly 90 countries around the world. Countries are excluded from the analysis only for reasons of data availability. The basis for this calculation is expression (3.2) in the formal model.

Table 3.3 presents these wealth figures for the selected Latin American countries of the preceding tables. While the net (genuine) savings figures are presented in per capita terms, it must be borne in mind that they refer to G/N and not G_N in the theoretical model. The latter is measured in the column headed 'change in wealth per capita'.

This table tells a rich story. First, comparing with Table 3.2, we see five countries – Bolivia, Colombia, Guatemala, Nicaragua and Paraguay – where total genuine saving is positive but the change in wealth per capita is negative. Population growth is swamping saving effort in these countries. Second, the loss in wealth per capita is truly significant in Ecuador and Venezuela, in sharp contrast to the robust gains in Chile and Uruguay.

In terms of the sensitivity of these results to the measured or assumed values of key parameters, it is clear, as in Hamilton (2003), that the population growth rate is an extremely sensitive variable. It is easy to see why this is true. Denoting total genuine saving by G and total wealth by

Table 3.2   Composition of genuine saving in selected countries, 1999, % of GNI

	Gross national saving	Education	Health	Consumption of fixed capital	Mineral depletion	Energy depletion	Net forest depletion	CO$_2$ damage	Net (genuine) saving
Argentina	14.0	3.2	3.3	14.6	0.0	0.2	0.0	0.3	5.4
Bolivia	10.9	5.5	7.0	11.8	0.6	0.5	0.0	0.9	9.6
Brazil	16.6	4.8	8.2	16.4	0.8	1.1	0.0	0.4	11.0
Chile	21.7	3.4	5.7	8.6	3.4	0.1	0.0	0.5	18.3
Colombia	11.5	3.1	11.4	14.7	0.0	5.2	0.0	0.5	5.6
Costa Rica	13.4	5.1	6.7	12.0	0.0	0.0	0.5	0.3	12.4
Ecuador	24.9	3.2	4.3	21.8	0.0	11.0	0.0	0.8	-1.3
El Salvador	14.6	2.2	7.2	11.4	0.0	0.0	0.8	0.3	11.5
Guatemala	11.9	1.5	4.8	10.4	0.0	0.7	1.0	0.3	5.8
Honduras	28.4	3.5	8.8	17.1	0.0	0.0	0.0	0.5	23.0
Mexico	21.1	4.5	4.9	18.0	0.0	3.7	0.0	0.5	8.2
Nicaragua	10.0	2.6	13.6	9.5	0.0	0.0	0.2	1.1	15.5
Paraguay	11.9	3.5	5.9	15.1	0.0	0.0	0.0	0.3	5.8
Peru	18.6	2.6	7.1	14.6	0.9	0.5	0.0	0.3	12.0
Uruguay	13.0	3.0	4.1	11.5	0.0	0.0	0.3	0.2	8.1
Venezuela, RB	22.2	5.0	4.0	21.2	0.2	16.3	0.0	1.0	-7.5

Table 3.3 Change in wealth per capita, selected countries, 1999

	GNI per capita ($)	Pop. growth (%)	Net saving per capita ($)	Wealth per capita ($)	Change in wealth per capita ($)	Change in wealth (% of total)
Argentina	7 539	1.3	410	22 711	126	0.6
Bolivia	991	2.3	95	4 486	–10	–0.2
Brazil	3 033	1.3	332	12 619	168	1.3
Chile	4 384	1.3	802	16 774	582	3.5
Colombia	1 983	1.8	111	9 265	–54	–0.6
Costa Rica	3 712	2.1	461	13 696	172	1.3
Ecuador	1 383	1.9	–18	8 395	–180	–2.1
El Salvador	1 976	1.9	227	6 612	98	1.5
Guatemala	1 627	2.6	95	7 360	–100	–1.4
Honduras	841	2.6	193	4 398	80	1.8
Mexico	4 827	1.4	397	22 055	90	0.4
Nicaragua	396	2.7	62	3 284	–26	–0.8
Paraguay	1 450	2.6	85	8 680	–145	–1.7
Peru	1 982	1.7	237	7 753	104	1.3
Uruguay	6 145	0.7	499	16 145	381	2.4
Venezuela, RB	4 294	2.0	–324	28 320	–884	–3.1

W_T, the elasticity ε of the change in wealth per capita G_N with respect to population growth rate g is given by,

$$\varepsilon = -\frac{g}{G/W_T - g}.$$

If G is 10 per cent of GNI while W_T is six times GNI, their ratio is of the same order of magnitude as the population growth rate g. Small variations in the latter will produce large variations in the estimated change in wealth per capita.

SUMMARY OF RESULTS

As noted above, the complete results of the calculation of changes in wealth per capita appear in Table 3A.1. This section employs a series of scatter diagrams to shed light on some of the key relationships underlying the country-level results.

Figure 3.1 displays the relationship between GNI per capita and the percentage change in wealth per capita. Note the logarithmic scale for GNI per capita. There is a clear upward trend in these figures – poorer countries have lower changes in wealth per capita. In fact, virtually all countries below $1000 per capita income exhibit declines in wealth per capita. The exceptions fall into two clusters. The right-most trio (around $800 GNI per capita) consists of China, Honduras and Sri Lanka. The next trio (around $400 per capita) consists of India, Zimbabwe and Bangladesh. The upper-right outlier is Singapore.

Figure 3.2 displays the relationship between total genuine saving, as a percentage of GNI, and the percentage change in wealth per capita. The upward trend here is unsurprising. However, one of the key questions posed in the introduction now has an answer: there are in fact a dozen countries in the sample where total genuine saving is positive but wealth per capita is declining. As seen in Table 3.3, five of these countries are in Latin America. The right-most point in the lower-right quadrant is Nicaragua.

Figure 3.3 displays the relationship between the percentage change in wealth per capita and the population growth rate. Here the trend is clearly downward: the higher the population growth rate, the lower the change in wealth per capita. But there is nothing inherently Malthusian in this result – there is a significant cluster of countries with population growth rates in excess of 1.5 per cent per year and positive changes in wealth. The right-most countries in this cluster are Jordan, Honduras, Malaysia and Costa Rica.

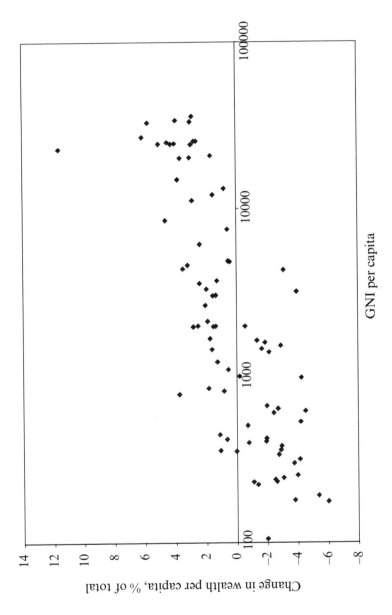

Figure 3.1 Percentage change in wealth per capita vs GNI per capita, 1999

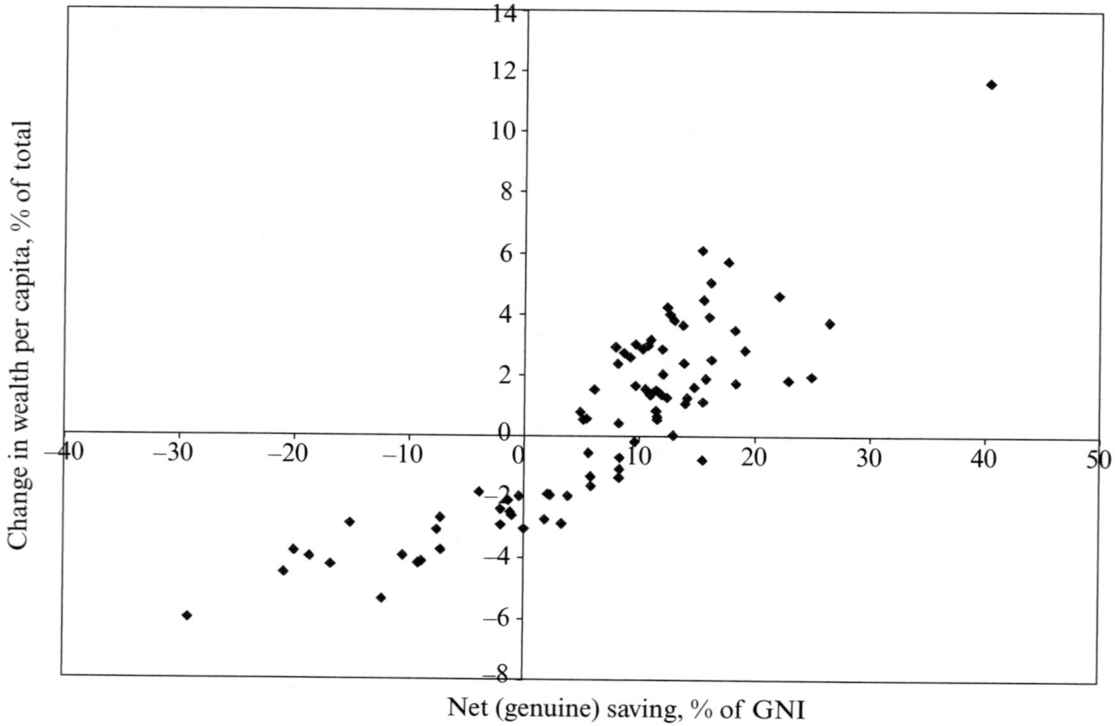

Figure 3.2   Percentage change in wealth per capita vs genuine saving rate, 1999

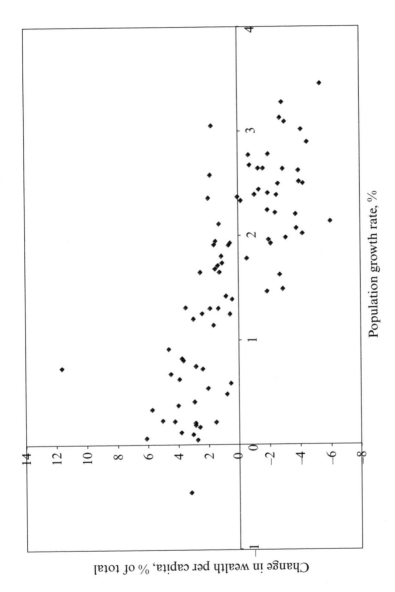

Figure 3.3   Percentage change in wealth per capita vs population growth rate, 1999

29

Finally, expression (3.2) for the change in wealth per capita can be exploited to calculate how high savings would have to be in order to move a country from negative to positive change in wealth per capita. For total (not per capita) genuine saving G and total wealth W_T, expression (3.2) can be written as,

$$G/N - g \cdot W_T/N \, .$$

The 'break-even' level of saving is therefore just the population growth rate times total wealth. The difference between the break-even level of saving and the actual level of saving, for countries where the change in wealth per capita is negative, is shown in Table 3A.1 as the 'savings gap' as a percentage of GNI. It is clearly enormous for some countries.

POTENTIAL CRITICISMS OF THE METHODOLOGY

Aside from the obvious issue of the number of assumptions that are stacked one upon the other in order to arrive at these changes in wealth estimates, there are two other concerns that need to be discussed.

First, as Weitzman and Löfgren (1997) show, *exogenous* technological change can add substantially to saving. While this result is significant for the United States and, presumably, for other advanced economies, it relies upon technological change being a completely exogenous process. If technological change is endogenous, then it is straightforward to show that there is no adjustment required to saving rates, other than to treat R&D expenditures as investment. At any event, technological change in developing countries, as measured by growth in total factor productivity, is a much smaller factor than in the developed world. Chapter 8 presents and discusses these important issues in greater detail.

Second, it is worth considering how *endogenous* processes of population growth could be modelled. This would typically proceed by specifying the population growth rate to be a declining function of wealth per capita (along with other possible determinants of fertility). In such a model a decline in wealth per capita could therefore lead a country into a poverty trap, owing to the increasing population growth rates that the model would entail. Similarly, increasing wealth per capita could lead to a virtuous circle of declining birth rates and accumulation of wealth per capita. It seems clear that any such model of endogenous population growth would accentuate the results derived in this chapter.

CONCLUSIONS

The first conclusion is a cautionary note on the cross-country values of wealth per capita in Table 3A.1. Because nominal exchange rates are used, this produces absurdities such as Japan appearing to be 60 per cent wealthier per capita than the United States. The figures presented are therefore useful for analysing percentage changes in wealth per capita within countries, but dollar figures should not be compared across countries – for this a PPP adjustment would be preferred.

The broad conclusion from this analysis is clear from Table 3A.1 and Figure 3.1. There is evidence to suggest that the majority of countries lying below median income per capita are accumulating total wealth – physical capital, natural resources, human capital, human health – at a rate lower than the rate of population growth. In fact, of the countries with less than $1000 per capita income, all exhibit negative change in wealth per capita, with China, Honduras, Sri Lanka, India, Zimbabwe and Bangladesh being the exceptions. While there is ample scope to achieve higher economic output from existing assets, by giving greater scope to markets and developing the institutions that support the operation of markets, this trend in total wealth per capita is ultimately not sustainable.

If the wealth and saving estimates are reasonable and population growth rates are given, then the savings gap figures in Table 3A.1 suggest that truly heroic increases in savings rates would be required to bring many countries onto a sustainable path. Malawi would have to save an additional 45 per cent of GNI, for example. If achieving these rates of saving is impractical, then the remaining policy levers must include those pertaining to population growth.

Figure 3.3, relating percentage changes in wealth per capita to population growth rates, has a distinctly Malthusian look to it. Note, however, that there is nothing inherently Malthusian in the model of wealth and welfare – increased saving effort and more effective investments can offset population growth. The national-level relationship in Figure 3.3 is consistent with the sort of spiral of resource degradation, poverty and population increase that Dasgupta (2000) postulates at the village level, but it is not a pre-ordained outcome.

Expression (3.3) makes it clear why this measure of change in wealth per capita is important for tracking development progress. To know whether the present value of utility per capita is increasing, it is sufficient to measure the change in real wealth per capita. Declines in this wealth figure imply not only declining development prospects, in terms of the present value of utility, but also unsustainability.

Hamilton and Clemens (1999) discuss the policies needed to boost genuine savings, spanning macroeconomic policies, investments in human capital, and policies to increase the efficiency with which the environment is used. But the bottom line is that reducing population growth must also play an important role in launching many countries onto a sustainable path. The positive agenda for reducing population growth involves such key elements as increasing female education and reducing infant and child mortality, which can yield very substantial social and economic benefits as byproducts.

NOTES

1. Nor does genuine saving, as set out here, speak to the question of technological change – an issue which is addressed in Chapter 8.
2. The genuine savings estimates published by the World Bank are kept up to date, but conceptual differences with the wealth estimates preclude simply updating the 1994 wealth estimates by accumulating the annual levels of genuine saving.
3. Hamilton (2003) uses total wealth in estimating the change in wealth per capita. A more complete specification of the underlying growth model, presented here, suggests that only tangible assets and human capital should be used in the calculation.
4. Genuine saving per capita will generally be termed 'change in wealth per capita' in what follows.

APPENDIX 3A.1: PER CAPITA SAVING AND PROSPECTS FOR DEVELOPMENT

For asset shadow prices γ_i, the current value Hamiltonian for the growth problem of expression (3.1) is,

$$H = u + \gamma_k \dot{k} + \gamma_s \dot{s} + \gamma_a \dot{a}$$
$$= u + \gamma_k \left(f - c - e - \delta k - gk \right) + \gamma_s \left(-q - gs \right) + \gamma_a \left(w - ga \right)$$

The static first-order conditions for a maximum serve to define the shadow prices:

$$\frac{\partial H}{\partial c} = 0 = u_c - \gamma_k \Rightarrow \gamma_k = u_c$$

$$\frac{\partial H}{\partial q} = 0 = \gamma_k F_R - \gamma_s \Rightarrow \gamma_s = u_c F_R$$

$$\frac{\partial H}{\partial e} = 0 = -\gamma_k + w_e \gamma_a \Rightarrow \gamma_a = \frac{u_c}{w_e} = u_c m$$

In the latter expression m is the marginal cost of creating a unit of human capital. Now define,

$$n = f - c - e - \delta k = \text{net investment per capita in produced capital.}$$

The Hamiltonian may now be expressed as,

$$H = u + u_c \left[\left(n - F_R q + mw \right) - g \left(k + F_R s + ma \right) \right] \qquad (3A.1)$$

The term in square brackets is the change in the real value of assets, or 'genuine' saving G_N. It is a well-known property of the Hamiltonian that,

$$H = \rho v.$$

Since $\dot{v} = \rho v - u$ it therefore follows from expression (3A.1) that

$$u_c G_N = \dot{v}.$$

APPENDIX 3A.2

Table 3A.1 Wealth and change in wealth per capita, 1999

	GNI per capita ($)	Pop growth (%)	Net saving per capita ($)	Wealth per capita ($)	Change in wealth per capita ($)	Change in wealth (% of total)	Saving gap (% GNI)
Algeria	1513	1.5	-228	15985	-466	-2.9	30.8
Argentina	7539	1.3	410	22711	126	0.6	..
Australia	20871	1.1	2024	72644	1192	1.6	..
Austria	25530	0.2	2351	85789	2204	2.6	..
Bangladesh	356	1.7	50	1782	19	1.1	..
Belgium	24525	0.2	3049	68640	2894	4.2	..
Benin	379	2.6	-7	2358	-70	-3.0	18.4
Bolivia	991	2.3	95	4486	-10	-0.2	1.0
Brazil	3033	1.3	332	12619	168	1.3	..
Burkina Faso	223	2.4	18	1753	-24	-1.4	11.0
Burundi	105	2.0	0	758	-15	-2.0	14.5
Cameroon	599	2.2	-12	5257	-129	-2.4	21.5
Canada	20181	0.8	2783	62673	2276	3.6	..
Chile	4384	1.3	802	16774	582	3.5	..
China	776	0.8	206	4518	168	3.7	..
Colombia	1983	1.8	111	9265	-54	-0.6	2.7
Congo, Rep.	613	2.9	-127	7747	-352	-4.5	57.4
Costa Rica	3712	2.1	461	13696	172	1.3	..

Côte d'Ivoire	660	2.8	25	3249	-65	-2.0	9.8
Denmark	32997	0.3	5836	96507	5509	5.7	:
Dominican Republic	1988	1.7	323	7806	194	2.5	:
Ecuador	1383	1.9	-18	8395	-180	-2.1	13.0
Egypt, Arab Rep.	1437	1.9	212	6059	96	1.6	:
El Salvador	1976	1.9	227	6612	98	1.5	:
Finland	24531	0.2	3970	75449	3794	5.0	:
France	24700	0.4	3122	71513	2851	4.0	:
Gabon	3181	2.6	-332	24660	-979	-4.0	:
Gambia, The	336	3.1	6	1753	-49	-2.8	30.8
Germany	25521	0.0	2203	79761	2164	2.7	14.5
Ghana	403	2.2	8	2843	-55	-1.9	13.7
Greece	12157	0.2	743	43140	649	1.5	:
Guatemala	1627	2.6	95	7360	-100	-1.4	6.2
Guinea-Bissau	179	2.1	-36	2030	-78	-3.8	43.4
Haiti	528	2.0	-48	2192	-92	-4.2	17.5
Honduras	841	2.6	193	4398	80	1.8	:
Hungary	4610	-0.5	508	18777	594	3.2	:
India	443	1.8	69	2367	26	1.1	:
Indonesia	634	1.6	-46	4148	-113	-2.7	17.9
Iran, Islamic Rep.	1583	1.5	-61	14544	-274	-1.9	17.3
Italy	20328	0.1	1974	63527	1910	3.0	:
Jamaica	2641	0.5	319	12460	251	2.0	:
Japan	35970	0.2	4319	142756	4048	2.8	:
Jordan	1671	3.1	307	6441	111	1.7	:
Kenya	352	2.4	46	1919	0	0.0	:

Table 3A.1 (continued)

	GNI per capita ($)	Pop growth (%)	Net saving per capita ($)	Wealth per capita ($)	Change in wealth per capita ($)	Change in wealth (% of total)	Saving gap (% GNI)
Korea, Rep.	8 556	0.9	1 894	34 345	1 579	4.6	..
Madagascar	244	3.1	0	1 168	–36	–3.1	14.7
Malawi	176	2.1	–51	1 317	–79	–6.0	45.1
Malaysia	3 308	2.4	827	19 200	373	1.9	..
Mali	239	2.4	–3	1 889	–48	–2.5	20.1
Mauritania	359	3.3	12	3 260	–95	–2.9	26.4
Mauritius	3 575	1.3	496	13 627	325	2.4	..
Mexico	4 827	1.4	397	22 055	90	0.4	..
Morocco	1 209	1.7	171	5 942	73	1.2	..
Nepal	231	2.4	19	1 493	–17	–1.1	7.2
Netherlands	25 112	0.7	3 914	76 141	3 397	4.5	..
New Zealand	13 274	0.5	649	51 553	398	0.8	..
Nicaragua	396	2.7	62	3 284	–26	–0.8	6.6
Niger	191	3.5	–23	1 206	–65	–5.4	34.1
Nigeria	253	2.5	–47	3 154	–126	–4.0	50.0
Norway	43 041	0.6	5 467	120 607	4 707	3.9	..
Pakistan	421	2.4	10	2 258	–45	–2.0	10.6
Paraguay	1 450	2.6	85	8 680	–145	–1.7	10.0
Peru	1 982	1.7	237	7 753	104	1.3	..
Philippines	1 088	1.9	126	5 114	27	0.5	..

Portugal	11 248	0.2	1 158	37 887	1 078	2.8	::
Rwanda	232	2.5	−2	1 653	−44	−2.6	18.8
Senegal	502	2.8	42	2 042	−15	−0.7	3.0
Singapore	22 892	0.7	9 238	74 803	8 687	11.6	::
South Africa	3 017	1.7	319	9 937	151	1.5	::
Spain	15 028	0.1	1 956	49 947	1 896	3.8	::
Sri Lanka	809	1.4	93	4 166	34	0.8	::
Sweden	26 978	0.1	4 153	67 540	4 111	6.1	::
Syrian Arab Rep.	971	2.5	−162	9 184	−392	−4.3	40.4
Thailand	1 970	0.8	377	10 604	298	2.8	::
Togo	315	3.0	−28	2 442	−101	−4.2	32.2
Trinidad & Tobago	4 882	0.6	252	22 723	118	0.5	::
Tunisia	2 122	1.3	335	10 583	197	1.9	::
United Kingdom	24 391	0.4	1 936	58 277	1 695	2.9	::
United States	33 418	1.2	3 597	86 255	2 557	3.0	::
Uruguay	6 145	0.7	499	16 145	381	2.4	::
Venezuela, RB	4 294	2.0	−324	28 320	−884	−3.1	20.6
Zambia	298	2.2	−21	1 363	−51	−3.8	17.3
Zimbabwe	416	1.9	48	1 896	12	0.6	::

Note: The saving gap is the increase in the share of GNI that would need to be saved in order to achieve zero change in wealth per capita.

4. Testing genuine saving

INTRODUCTION

Intuition suggests that saving today should have an effect on future economic performance, and indeed the large body of work on cross-country analysis of economic growth supports this (see, for example, Sala-i-Martin, 1997). As shown in Chapter 2, this intuition was made formal in Hamilton and Clemens (1999), where it was reported that current net or genuine saving is precisely equal to the change in the present value of future utility along the optimal development path for an economy. The work has been extended by Dasgupta and Mäler (2000) and Asheim and Weitzman (2001). This theory can provide a basic framework for testing, using historical data, whether current saving does in fact predict future changes in welfare. Recent papers by Ferreira and Vincent (2005) and Ferreira et al. (2003) have explored the question in detail. This chapter provides an alternative framework and empirical test.

A key motivation for an alternative test lies in the restrictiveness of the assumptions underlying other frameworks. For example, the very general model of Weitzman (1976) requires (i) that the economy be on the optimal path which maximizes the present value of consumption and (ii) that the interest rate be constant. These are both strong assumptions. The model of Ferreira et al. (2003) presents other problems for estimation, as the following simple two-stock model demonstrates.

Assume a Dasgupta–Heal type economy with a finite stock of resource S which is extracted at rate R, and where production depends on the capital stock and flow of resources, that is, $F = F(K, R)$. We assume constant returns to scale. The basic accounting identities for the economy are:

$$\dot{K} = F(K, R) - C$$
$$S = \int_t^{\infty} R(s)\, ds$$
$$\dot{S} = -R.$$

Assuming profit maximization, the price of the resource is given by F_R, which must satisfy the usual arbitrage relationship (the Hotelling rule),

$$\dot{F}_R / F_R = F_K,$$

while F_K is the interest rate for the economy. Total wealth is defined as,

$$W = K + \int_t^\infty F_R(s) R(s) \cdot \exp\left(-\int_t^s F_K(\tau) d\tau\right) ds = K + F_R S.$$

These basic relationships plus constant returns to scale lead to the following derivation:

$$\begin{aligned} C &= F - \dot{K} + \dot{F}_R S - \dot{F}_R S \\ &= F_K K + F_R R - \dot{K} + F_K F_R S - \dot{F}_R S \\ &= F_K (K + F_R S) - \dot{K} - F_R \dot{S} - \dot{F}_R S \\ &= F_K W - \dot{W}. \end{aligned} \qquad (4.1)$$

This differential equation has a particular solution,

$$W = \int_t^\infty C(s) \cdot \exp\left(-\int_t^s F_K(\tau) d\tau\right) ds,$$

so wealth is just the present value of consumption along the profit-maximizing path.

Since genuine saving for this economy is given by $G \equiv \dot{K} - F_R R$, expression (4.1) can be rewritten as,

$$F_K \int_t^\infty C(s) \cdot \exp\left(-\int_t^s F_K(\tau) d\tau\right) ds - C = G + \dot{F}_R S. \qquad (4.2)$$

This is the expression tested by Ferreira et al. (2003) – genuine saving plus capital gains at time t should equal the difference between a particular average of future consumption and current consumption. This approach to the problem entails two restrictive assumptions, (i) profit maximization and (ii) constant returns to scale, and encounters one considerable practical problem, the measurement of capital gains. Although expression (4.2) shows only capital gains on the exhaustible resource, a more general model would suggest that all capital gains should be included – however, cross-country time series data on capital gains are lacking.

An alternative approach to testing genuine saving may be derived from Hamilton and Hartwick (2005). For the same profit-maximizing model,

$$\dot{C} = \dot{F} - \ddot{K} - \dot{F}_R R + \dot{F}_R R$$
$$= F_K \dot{K} - F_K F_R R - \ddot{K} + F_R \dot{R} + \dot{F}_R R$$
$$= F_K G - \dot{G}.$$

This has a particular solution,

$$\int_t^\infty \dot{C}(s) \cdot \exp\left(-\int_t^s F_K(\tau) d\tau\right) ds = G, \qquad (4.3)$$

which provides the basic test of saving employed below: current genuine saving should equal the present value of future changes in consumption. This is a more parsimonious model, requiring only profit maximization. In the more general model of Chapter 2, if utility depends only on consumption, then expression (2.7) leads to precisely the same expression relating current saving and changes in future consumption – as Hamilton and Withagen (forthcoming) show, this result for the general model requires that the economy be competitive (households maximize utility while producers maximize profits) and that any externalities be internalized through Pigouvian taxes.

As in Ferreira et al. (2003), the econometric test of saving which we wish to apply is,

$$PVC_i = \alpha + \beta \cdot G_i + \varepsilon_i, \qquad (4.4)$$

where G_i is one of several alternative measures of saving, while PVC_i is the present value of changes in future consumption for country i. If the data fit the theory, then we would expect $\alpha = 0$ and $\beta = 1$.

We need to account for population growth when measuring saving, as shown in Chapter 3. Therefore to the model of Chapter 2 we add population N assumed to be growing at exogenous rate g; GDP is denoted Y. The key variables to be subjected to econometric analysis are therefore calculated in the base period ($t = 0$) as,

$$PVC_0 = \left(\frac{Y_0}{N_0}\right)^{-1} \sum_{j=1}^{T} \left(\frac{C_j/N_j - C_{j-1}/N_{j-1}}{(1+r)^j}\right)$$

$$G_0 = \left(\frac{Y_0}{N_0}\right)^{-1} \left(\frac{(Y_0 - C_0) - \delta K_0 + \sum p_{i0} \dot{X}_{i0}}{N_0} - g \cdot \frac{(K_0 + \sum p_{i0} X_{i0})}{N_0}\right).$$

Here δK_0 is depreciation of produced assets, while pi_0 is the shadow price of the i-th asset. Both expressions are normalized to current GDP per capita for expositional purposes. The four alternative measures of saving which we test are:

1. Gross saving $= \left(\dfrac{Y_0}{N_0}\right)^{-1}\left(\dfrac{(Y_0 - C_0)}{N_0}\right).$

2. Net saving $= \left(\dfrac{Y_0}{N_0}\right)^{-1}\left(\dfrac{(Y_0 - C_0) - \delta K_0}{N_0}\right).$

3. Genuine saving $= \left(\dfrac{Y_0}{N_0}\right)^{-1}\left(\dfrac{(Y_0 - C_0) - \delta K_0 + \sum p_{i0}\dot{X}_{i0}}{N_0}\right).$

4. Malthusian saving $= \left(\dfrac{Y_0}{N_0}\right)^{-1}\left(\begin{array}{c}\dfrac{(Y_0 - C_0) - \delta K_0 + \sum p_{i0}\dot{X}_{i0}}{N_0} \\ -g \cdot \dfrac{(K_0 + \sum p_{i0}X_{i0})}{N_0}\end{array}\right).$

We term the fourth measure 'Malthusian' saving owing to the final term reflecting the immiserating effects of population growth.

DATA

All data for the analysis – GDP, gross saving, consumption of fixed capital,[1] and depletion of natural resources (energy, minerals and net forest depletion) – are taken directly from the *World Development Indicators* (World Bank, 2002a). Total wealth, employed in the Malthusian saving calculation, is derived as shown in Chapter 3, with a perpetual inventory model for produced capital stock estimates, present values of mineral and energy rents, and present values of forestry, fishing and agricultural rents, all measured in constant 1995 dollars, providing the basic estimates. These are the same total wealth data employed in Ferreira et al. (2003).

As in Ferreira and Vincent (2005) and Ferreira et al. (2003), we exclude public expenditures on education from the saving measures – these were shown to perform exceedingly badly in the earlier work. There are a number of plausible reasons for the poor performance: (i) these are gross, rather than net, investment estimates; (ii) private expenditures are excluded; and (iii) expenditures may be a particularly poor proxy for human capital formation, particularly in developing countries (see Pritchett, 1996).

We also exclude damages from CO_2 emissions. This is partly because the bulk of the damages occur in the longer term, but mostly because damages to other countries (the major effect of emitting CO_2) should have no effect on future consumption in the emitting country in the absence of a binding agreement to pay compensation.

METHODOLOGY FOR ESTIMATION

One of the key choices to be made in estimating expression (4.4) is the choice of period over which to calculate changes in consumption. The underlying theory, as expressed in (4.3), suggests that there is in principle an infinite time horizon. As a practical matter, however, the *WDI* data on genuine savings are limited to the period 1970–2000, with data for the early 1970s being particularly sparse.

A reasonable choice of time horizon would be the mean lifetime of produced capital stocks, roughly 20 years (machinery and equipment lifetimes are typically shorter, 10 years or so, but buildings and infrastructure have lifetimes of several decades). Choosing 20 years would be saying, in effect, that the effects of savings will be felt over the lifetime of the produced capital in which they are presumed to be invested. This is the assumption used below, and testing the estimation for a 10-year time horizon produced less robust estimates overall (in terms of explained variation, probability of rejecting a linear relationship between dependent and independent variables, and significance of the coefficients on saving).

The other decision required for estimation concerns the discount rate. The underlying theory (see Chapter 3 and Ferreira et al., 2003) suggests that the rate should be the marginal product of capital less depreciation rates for produced capital, less population growth rates, which argues for a low value. We use a uniform rate of 5 per cent, and tests of alternatives suggest that the estimates are fairly insensitive to small changes in the discount rate.

Allowing for the sparse early 1970s savings data,[2] therefore, expression (4.4) was estimated using ordinary least squares (OLS) for consecutive 20-year periods from 1976–1980. In other words, what we are asking using this method is how well does cross-country performance for a specific saving measure in, say 1976, predict changes in consumption levels up to 1996 and so on. These results, as well as more informal methods, are reported below.

EMPIRICAL RESULTS

To give a feel for the data, we first scatter the present value of changes in consumption against the four different savings measures for 1980 in Figures 4.1–4.4. The broad picture which emerges is that there is no monotonic improvement in the fit with theory as more stringent measures of saving are applied. The coefficient on saving actually drops moving from gross saving to net saving, and the explained variation drops considerably. For genuine saving the coefficient on saving is very near 1 and the explained variation is the highest of the four saving measures. Finally, for Malthusian saving the coefficient on saving drops to the lowest level of the four measures, while explained variation reaches its highest value.

Figure 4.5 presents the same scatter for high income countries only. As seen in Ferreira and Vincent (2005) and Ferreira et al. (2003), the model fit is particularly poor for these countries – further tests show the coefficient on saving to be insignificant, while the explained variation is very low.

Table 4.1 presents the results of the individual OLS estimates of the model for each of the five years and four measures of saving. This table reports the coefficient values with t-statistics, R-squared, degrees of freedom, the probability of rejecting a linear relationship (from the F statistic) and a simple two-sided t-test of whether the coefficient on saving is equal to 1 (values greater than 2.00 imply the coefficient is significantly different from 1 at the 5 per cent confidence level).

While there is some heterogeneity in the results, the following broad conclusions hold:

- The results for 1977 are the weakest of the five years, with low R-squared, higher probabilities of rejecting a linear relationship than other years and two saving coefficient estimates that are significantly different from 1 (although the coefficient for net saving is not itself significant). This suggests some systematic shock being picked up by the data for this year.
- Results for net saving are generally the weakest of the four saving measures tested, with insignificant coefficients on saving at the 5 per cent level in 1976 and 1977, and generally low R-squared and higher probability of rejecting a linear relationship than other measures.
- Malthusian saving exhibits the worst fit with theory, with the coefficients on saving being the lowest of the four saving measures, and significantly different from 1 in four out of the five years tested.
- The results for gross and genuine saving have similarities, with the coefficients on saving being significant and not significantly different from 1 in all years. Genuine saving explains much more of the total

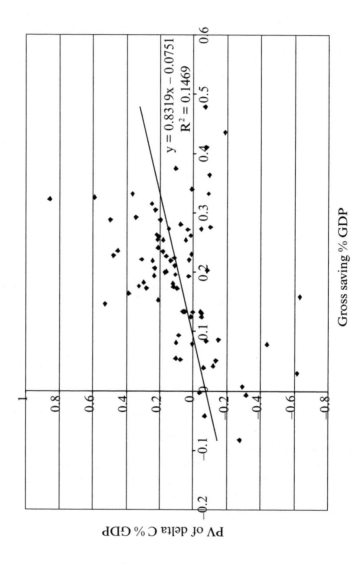

Figure 4.1   PV of change in consumption vs gross saving, 1980

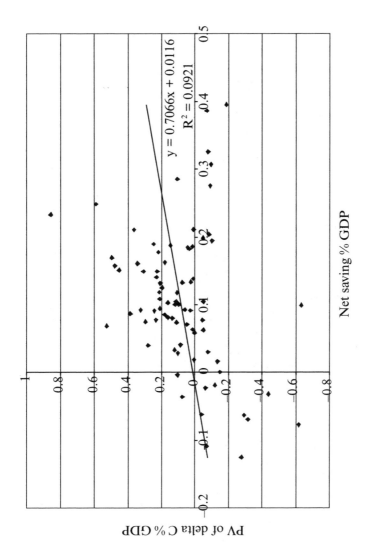

Figure 4.2 PV of change in consumption vs net saving, 1980

45

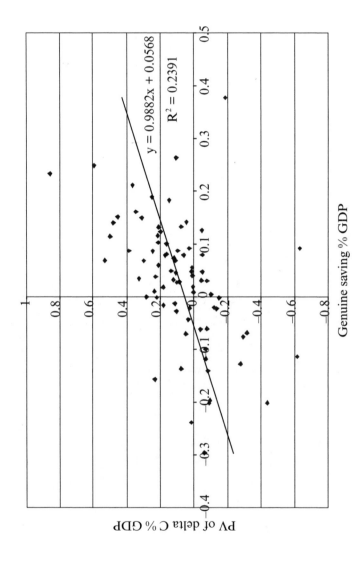

Figure 4.3   *PV of change in consumption vs genuine saving, 1980*

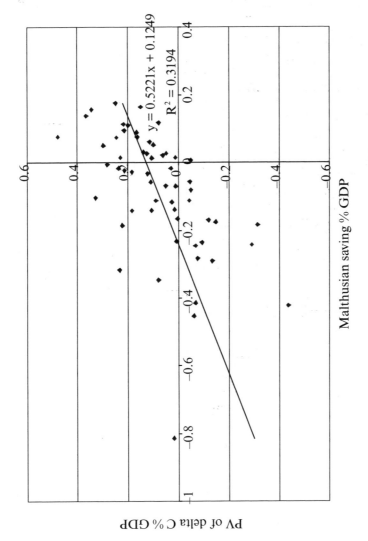

$y = 0.5221x + 0.1249$

$R^2 = 0.3194$

PV of delta C % GDP

Malthusian saving % GDP

Figure 4.4   PV of change in consumption vs Malthusian saving, 1980

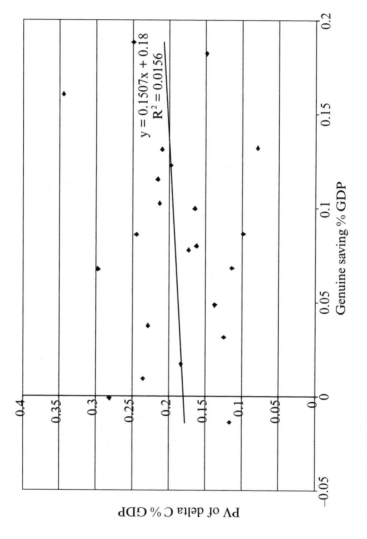

Figure 4.5   PV of change in consumption vs genuine saving, high income countries, 1980

Table 4.1 Regression results for PVC = alpha + beta * Saving

	1976		1977		1978		1979		1980	
	beta	alpha	beta	alpha	beta	alpha	beta	alpha	beta	alpha
Gross saving										
Coeff.	1.0152	-0.0737	0.7596	-0.0338	1.0484	-0.1212	1.2325	-0.1743	0.8319	-0.0751
tstat	3.0335	-0.9511	2.4358	-0.4628	3.7257	-1.8992	4.7372	-2.8601	3.6416	-1.4656
Rsq	0.1479		0.0803		0.1598		0.2351		0.1469	
Df	53		68		73		73		77	
Pr > F	0.0037		0.0175		0.0004		0.0000		0.0005	
beta = 1	0.0445		-0.7595		0.1697		0.8814		-0.7264	
Net saving										
Coeff.	0.6634	0.0606	0.2161	0.1047	0.6485	0.0209	0.9835	-0.0293	0.7066	0.0116
tstat	1.7723	1.0787	0.6471	2.0414	1.9740	0.4433	3.2791	-0.6574	2.7943	0.3102
Rsq	0.0560		0.0061		0.0507		0.1284		0.0921	
Df	53		68		73		73		77	
Pr > F	0.0821		0.5198		0.0522		0.0016		0.0066	
beta = 1	-0.8823		-2.3125		-1.0555		-0.0542		-1.1451	
Genuine saving										
Coeff.	1.2803	0.0483	0.8532	0.0677	1.2553	0.0131	0.7815	0.0580	0.9882	0.0568
tstat	4.5524	1.4442	3.4246	2.1915	4.9943	0.4654	4.2716	2.3469	4.9187	2.3175
Rsq	0.2811		0.1471		0.2547		0.2000		0.2391	
Df	53		68		73		73		77	
Pr > F	0.0000		0.0010		0.0000		0.0001		0.0000	
beta = 1	0.9780		-0.5808		1.0019		-1.1781		-0.0578	
Malthusian saving										
Coeff.	0.7757	0.1337	0.5741	0.1200	0.4663	0.1061	0.3599	0.1117	0.5221	0.1249
tstat	3.8801	5.1418	3.2489	5.0664	4.0371	5.0553	3.7425	5.2683	5.1265	6.1294
Rsq	0.2785		0.1772		0.2352		0.2030		0.3194	
Df	39		49		53		55		56	
Pr > F	0.0004		0.0021		0.0002		0.0004		0.0000	
beta = 1	-1.0937		-2.3613		-4.5343		-6.5358		-4.6100	

variation in four out of five years, and exhibits lower probability of rejecting a linear relationship in the same four years, suggesting a more robust fit with theory.

Quantitative analysis suggests a moderate advantage to using genuine saving as a 'predictor' of future welfare, in the sense of a 1 percentage change in saving translating into a 1 per cent change in the present value of changes in future consumption. Figures 4.1 and 4.3 suggest a more qualitative test. In Figure 4.1 it can clearly be seen that gross saving provides many 'false positives' in the form of positive base-year savings translating into negative welfare outcomes – these are the scatter points lying in the lower-right quadrant. Similarly, the upper-left quadrant points in Figure 4.3 represent 'false negatives' – countries where negative base-year genuine savings were associated with increases in welfare.

Table 4.2 assembles the proportions of false positives and false negatives[3] for all saving measures for all years, along with an average for each saving measure weighted by the number of countries with positive or negative savings observed. A few observations:

- Malthusian saving has the lowest proportion of false positives, but in fact the vast majority of the countries with positive Malthusian saving are developed countries – the result is therefore unsurprising. This saving measure also has the highest proportion of false negatives, which is consistent with the results of the quantitative analysis.
- Gross and net saving have relatively low proportions of false negatives, but this represents very few countries (only one in the case of gross saving) across all years. There are simply very few countries with negative gross or net saving.
- Genuine saving has lower proportions of false positives than either gross or net saving, but this is balanced by a much higher proportion of false negatives.

CONCLUSIONS

Growth theory provides the basis for a stringent test of whether saving does in fact translate into future welfare. This chapter confronts the theory with 'real world' data, with positive results at least for measures of gross and genuine saving. Even without appealing to theoretical models, it may be asked when a dollar is saved how it could *not* show up in future production and consumption. Many answers to this question are possible: (i) saving may be measured very badly; (ii) funds appropriated for public investments

Table 4.2   False signals regarding future changes in consumption (ratios)

	1976	1977	1978	1979	1980	Wt. avg.
Gross saving						
False positive	0.241	0.246	0.320	0.360	0.267	0.294
False negative	1.000	0.000	0.000	0.000	0.000	0.167
Net saving						
False positive	0.226	0.250	0.275	0.338	0.209	0.266
False negative	0.500	0.500	0.167	0.250	0.167	0.231
Genuine saving						
False positive	0.188	0.200	0.226	0.293	0.154	0.218
False negative	0.429	0.400	0.231	0.412	0.407	0.378
Malthusian saving						
False positive	0.043	0.080	0.037	0.077	0.043	0.056
False negative	0.611	0.615	0.464	0.452	0.600	0.543

may not in fact be invested, owing to problems of governance; and (iii) investments, particularly by the public sector, may not be productive.

It is important to note the many caveats pertaining to this analysis. First, measurement error may be significant, particularly for consumption of fixed capital (where government estimates may be incorrect), depletion of natural resources (where World Bank resource rent estimates depend on rather sparse cost of extraction data, and where the methodology probably inflates the value of depletion for countries with large resource deposits), and total wealth estimates (especially produced capital in developing countries, where public investments may be particularly inefficient; see Pritchett, 2000).

Missing variable bias may also be an issue. Although human capital is excluded from the analysis for the reasons outlined above, in principle net investment in human capital should be an important contributor to future welfare. However, the negative effects of including education spending in the analysis of saving and future welfare in Ferreira and Vincent (2005) and Ferreira et al. (2003) may simply be another manifestation of the small or negative growth impact of public education spending in developing countries analysed by Pritchett (1996). In addition, for some countries the exclusion of natural resources such as diamonds and fish may be a significant omission.

Exogenous shocks may present problems for testing the theory of saving and social welfare. The period under analysis in this chapter includes, in the early and least heavily discounted stages, the second oil shock in 1979 and a steep worldwide recession in 1981. However, Ferreira et al. (2003) do not find any significant effects of exchange rate shocks in their analysis of the theory.

Turning to the results of the analysis, we find that the various saving measures are poor at signalling future changes in welfare in developed countries, which is similar to the findings of Ferreira and Vincent (2005) and Ferreira et al. (2003). This probably reflects factors other than capital accumulation being key for the growth performance of these economies, in particular technological innovation. For all countries combined, we find that both net and Malthusian saving fit the theory poorly. The significantly low coefficients on Malthusian saving suggest that this measure overstates the effects of population growth on wealth accumulation per capita with possible implications then for interpreting the analysis in Chapter 3. Gross and genuine saving perform well, with estimated coefficients not being significantly different from the predicted values and with lower probabilities of rejecting a linear relationship between dependent and independent variables than for other measures. Genuine saving performs marginally better than gross saving in terms of goodness of fit.

In terms of the more qualitative question of false positives and negatives, genuine saving provides on average a lower false positive ratio than gross saving (22 per cent of countries with positive genuine saving at a point in time actually experienced welfare declines, compared with 29 per cent of countries with positive gross saving). Conversely, negative genuine saving falsely signalled future welfare decreases in 38 per cent of cases on average.

It should be noted that the theory being tested is particularly stringent, since it implies that measuring positive or negative saving *at a point in time* leads to future welfare being higher or lower than current welfare over some interval of time. In the real non-optimal world a positive exogenous shock (such as an improvement in the terms of trade) in the year immediately following the time when saving turned negative could easily swamp the effect of negative saving, and conversely for positive saving and negative shocks.

NOTES

1. Ferreira et al. (2003) use estimated figures for consumption of fixed capital derived from the perpetual inventory model used to estimate total stocks of produced capital. Inspection of these figures reveals a fairly large number of anomalous estimates.
2. From 1970 to 1975 there are fewer than 40 countries with the necessary data, and these are primarily developed countries.
3. This is clearly a rather ad hoc test, but one that policymakers may care about.

5. Resources, growth and the 'paradox of plenty'

INTRODUCTION[1]

The re-emergence of interest in the determinants of economic growth has provided a reminder that a range of policy-related variables can have a persistent influence on economic growth rates. Parallel contributions to the theory and measurement of sustainability have focused on the implications of imprudent use of natural resources and inefficient levels of environmental degradation for sustaining economic development. One important link between these two questions is the paradoxical but seemingly robust finding of a negative and significant relationship between natural resource and the growth rate of per capita gross domestic product (GDP). This finding has been characterized as confirming the 'resource curse hypothesis' or 'paradox of plenty'.

Not surprisingly, there has been considerable effort expended to understand why the resource curse arises and, more importantly, whether it can be avoided. The focus of this book on sustainability would suggest that the problem might lie in the mismanagement of the portfolio of assets of resource-abundant countries. That is, in practice, it appears that the prudent path of saving resource rents has been difficult to achieve. In this chapter, we explore further the links between some of those factors said to be important to understanding sustainability and the resource curse hypothesis. Using simple cross-country growth regressions, we examine this relationship using a direct measure of natural resource abundance: the share of resource rents in GDP for a range of natural resources including energy and mineral and timber resources. In doing so, we explore a number of factors related to the proposition that it is the inability of resource-rich economies to transform this natural good fortune into saving that explains the curse or the paradox.

THE RESOURCE CURSE AND SUSTAINABILITY

The proposition that, other things being equal, resource abundance (that is, natural wealth) should increase the level of per capita economic welfare that a country can sustain into the future is well known (see, for a review, Auty and Mikesell, 1998). These advantages are twofold. Firstly, the discovery and development of natural resources can lead to a short-term increase in the rate of economic growth. Secondly, the exploitation of a resource windfall raises the level of welfare that can be sustained into the future. In principle then it would appear that resource-rich countries have distinct economic advantages over (otherwise identical) resource-poor counterparts. However, there is now significant case-study evidence that, in practice, many resource-rich countries have not enjoyed these benefits (see, for example, Gelb and Associates, 1988; Auty, 2001). This pattern of development in the presence of resource abundance has become known as the resource curse hypothesis.

This finding has also been generalized across relatively large samples of countries beginning with Sachs and Warner (1995). This pioneering study found statistically significant evidence for a negative relationship between per capita economic growth and resource abundance, over the period 1970 to 1990, controlling for the effect of other economic and policy variables on economic growth (such as openness, quality of public institutions and regional specific influences). In contrast, however, Davis (1995) presents evidence that the curse is not necessarily an empirical generality. More recently, Stijns (2000) shows that further statistical probing of the relationship between resource abundance and economic development reveals the importance of relatively sophisticated mechanisms via which resource-rich countries might reap both costs and benefits as a result of their natural wealth.

The theory of sustainability, as outlined in earlier chapters, suggests that resource-abundant countries, which are interested in balancing the well-being of future and the present should pursue a policy of prudently saving and investing the rents from resource extraction. In effect, the paradox could arise from the fact that, in practice, many countries have found this prudence difficult to achieve (Gelb and Associates, 1988). Figure 5.1 plots the (simple) relationship between gross saving (measured by period average gross savings as a percentage of GDP over 1980–95) and resource depletion (measured by period average resource rents as a percentage of GDP over 1980–95 on a log scale). This appears to suggest that while resource abundance might be weakly associated with a higher savings effort at relatively high levels of abundance there is no straightforward relationship between resource depletion and savings.

To reiterate, theoretical interest in genuine saving is primarily motivated by the finding that (for constant population) the observation of negative genuine savings means that welfare per capita will decline along the path.[2] However, it can also be shown that negative genuine savings will also result in

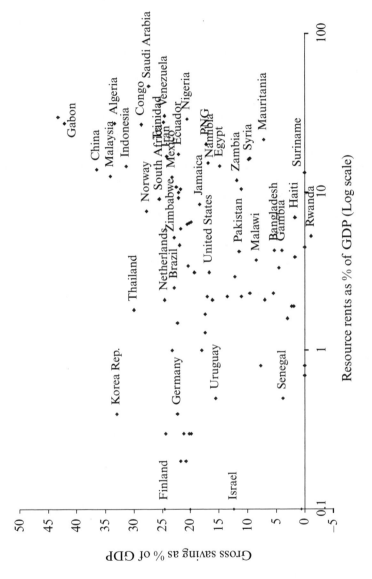

Figure 5.1 Resource depletion and gross saving, 1980–95

55

declining GDP (Hamilton, 1995) which is itself one outward manifestation of the curse or paradox. If there is indeed a robust and negative relationship between economic growth and natural resource abundance then clearly this begs the question regarding the circumstances under which this curse might develop. McMahon (1997), in an authoritative review of the literature, outlines a plethora of suggested mechanisms which can be characterized as based either on purely economic phenomena or on wider policy failures that cause resource rents to be dissipated (that is, in effect, wasted).

Economic explanations for the resource curse include 'Dutch disease' effects whereby a boom in the resource sector leads, via an overvalued exchange rate, to declining fortunes elsewhere in the traded economy, particularly the agricultural and manufacturing sectors (Corden and Neary, 1982). Furthermore, if the latter are characterized to a greater extent by economies of scale (for example, based on learning-by-doing) then relative decline could impact negatively on economic activity in the aggregate (Matsuyama, 1992). Sachs and Warner (1995, 2001) attribute their resource curse findings largely to 'Dutch-disease type' effects. A recent contribution by Gylfason (2001) has emphasized that resource abundance might have the effect of 'crowding out' the accumulation of one key engine of economic growth; namely, human capital. That is, dependence on natural wealth might somehow diminish incentives for resource abundant economies (either by accident or by design) to accumulate human capital via investments in education or knowledge sectors.[3]

Other studies have focused explicitly on the potential for policy failure and specifically the absence of effective institutions to reinvest productively the proceeds of resource depletion. For example, Gelb and Associates (1988) find that resource revenues are often committed by national governments to supporting existing political and economic institutions. Lane and Tornell (1996) attribute such outcomes to the submission of national governments to rampant rent-seeking behaviour by powerful interest groups within countries. This gives rise to a *voracity effect* whereby the growth benefits of (terms-of-trade) windfalls are dissipated by a combination of weak government and significant rent-seeking activity amongst competing societal groups.

In the remainder of this chapter, we focus primarily on those explanations of the resource curse hypothesis that suggest that resource abundance allows countries to retain 'bad' policies for longer than otherwise would be desirable or 'sustainable'. One effect of such policies might be persistently low (or even negative) genuine saving rates with adverse consequences for economic growth. Conversely, sound government policies combined with the prudent allocation of resources revenues to saving may enhance prospects that the discovery and exploitation of natural resources is transformed into sustained increases in income. In what follows we focus on this relationship between economic growth, the resource curse and saving via the statistical analysis of cross-country experience.

EMPIRICAL ANALYSIS

The framework for the empirical analysis of the determinants of economic growth determination is set out in Barro and Sala-i-Martin (1995). In practice, there are different approaches to this measurement problem some of which are explicitly based on extensions of the Solow neoclassical growth model while others focus upon reduced-form models (Temple, 1999; Aron, 1998). The key feature of all these approaches, however, is the inclusion of initial income in a cross-country regression that seeks to quantify the determinants of per capita income growth. The basis for this commonality is the idea of conditional convergence; that is, an economy will enjoy a faster growth rate the further it is from its own steady state value of output (Barro and Sala-i-Martin, 1995). Other growth determinants of possible interest include human capital or investment (in produced capital) and a range of policy variables such as government size and other factors of which resource abundance is just one candidate. For a comprehensive discussion of the findings and criticisms of cross-country growth regressions see Temple (1999).

DATA AND SCOPE OF ANALYSIS

Our data cover the period 1980 to 1995 and consist of initial period (1980) and period average data. All data are generated from World Bank (1999) and World Bank (1997) unless otherwise indicated. World Bank (1997) includes data on resource rents and genuine saving for a total of 103 countries, but given absences of data for other key variables our basic sample consists of 91 countries the details of which can be found in Appendix 5A.1. Our sample of countries, based primarily on World Bank (1997, 1999), includes a wide range of countries, as indicated in Appendix 5A.1, such as those which might be variously described as (some combination of) high, middle or low income (in per capita terms), resource-rich (for example, a relatively high share of rents in GDP) or resource-poor (for example, a relatively low or near zero share of rents in GDP).[4]

Resources analysed in what follows include oil, gas, coal, bauxite, copper, iron, lead, nickel, phosphate, tin, zinc, gold, silver and timber (forest resources). Total resource rent or depletion, for each of these resources, is defined as the product of a given resource's unit rent (that is, its world price minus country-specific extraction costs) and total units or quantity extracted (or harvested) in any year.[5] The share of all total resource rents in GDP is our chosen measure of resource abundance. Genuine savings rates are calculated here by subtracting the value of resource depletion from the net saving rate (that is, gross saving minus the depreciation of produced capital). A full list of the definitions of the variables used can be found in Appendix 5A.2.

It is worth noting that the definition of resource abundance used in this chapter is distinct from that elsewhere in the (statistical) literature on the link between resources and development. For example, Stijns (2000) focuses on only energy wealth while other studies such as Sachs and Warner (1995) (on exports of fuels, minerals and agricultural products) and Gylfason (2001) (on natural wealth including land rents) have interpreted resource abundance more broadly. The focus in the current chapter, however, is not on the totality of a country's resources. For example, we do not consider land rents in our measure of natural resource abundance. Rather the current emphasis is on the link between development and those (commercial) resources the depletion of which can be characterized as debits from genuine saving. In World Bank (1997) these resources include net timber accumulation as well as the depletion of energy and mineral resources. The rationale for this focus is that mismanagement of total rents arising from the liquidation of those living and non-living resources (for which data are available) might be suggestive of one mechanism whereby a 'resource curse' takes effect.[6]

As discussed in the previous chapters, the World Bank figures used here arguably overestimate the value of depletion. The reason for this is a lack of data on marginal extraction costs.[7] Alternative measures, such as the simple present value (or El Serafy) method, arguably however underestimate depletion by assuming no optimization of the extraction path. At any event, for modest stock sizes (say, 20 years' worth of production) and low social discount rates, the variance between the World Bank and other possible estimates of depletion are not huge. For substantially larger stock sizes, it is highly uncertain how valuable these resources will be in the future, which would argue for caution in blindly applying a simple present value approach. Put another way, unless it is thought that the long-term trend in resource prices will be constant then the assumption of constant rents under the present value method is likely to significantly under- or over-predict the value of these resources.

. A last point, before we turn to our findings, is that some contributions to the resource curse literature such as Sachs and Warner (1995) and Stijns (2000) have sought to develop 'formal' models, where others have sought, more simply, to evaluate the curse without reference to an explicit model as such. Clearly, the merits of the former approach are that a relatively sophisticated picture can potentially be built with respect to the role of resources and other variables, including possible direct and indirect pathways, on key development outcomes such as the GDP per capita growth rate. In the current chapter, while we do not motivate our empirical analysis with reference to formal models in this way, the discussion above indicates that the motivation for this analysis is the assertion, drawn from the sustainability and green national accounting literature, that while resource abundance is not inherently unsustainable, negative genuine saving is, in the sense that it leads (in certain circumstances) to declining welfare or GDP growth (for example, Chapter 2 or Hamilton, 1995). We take such findings to suggest three lines of enquiry. To the extent that a resource curse is indicated by the data that we analyse: (i) is the curse explained by government 'policy' that arguably leads to a reduction in the rate of genuine saving (for example, the financing of government consumption)? (ii) Have countries that have avoided negative genuine saving rates avoided the curse? (iii) To what extent have resource-abundant countries financed additional saving and investment using the proceeds of this natural wealth and has the existence of certain factors, such as high quality institutions, enhanced this saving and investment effort?

RESULTS

Table 5.1 reports key summary statistics for the whole sample and according to whether countries are classified as having above and below the mean share of resource rents in GDP (respectively, 'above' and 'equal to or below' a period average of 6.9 per cent of GDP). The table indicates that the GDP growth rate (*GDP8095*) was higher in countries with below mean rents (that is, these countries enjoyed, on average, more than 1 per cent higher growth than countries with above mean rents). In addition, countries with few resources also started the period with higher per capita income than their resource-rich counterparts. With respect to indicators of wealth accumulation, there is little apparent difference in the period average gross savings ratio (*SAVE*) or gross investment (*INV*) according to whether countries are resource-poor or resource-rich. It is interesting then to note that there does exist a wide disparity (of more than 10 per cent) between period average genuine savings (*GS*) according to the resource abundance category into which countries fall. That is, genuine savings are negative (on average, –2.6 per cent of GDP) in resource-rich countries and are positive (on average, 9.2 per cent of GDP) in resource-poor countries. These summary data seem to be at least suggestive of mixed fortunes according to whether countries are resource abundant, especially with regard to economic growth and genuine saving experience.

Table 5.1   Summary statistics

	Full sample	$RENT \leq 0.069$	$RENT > 0.069$
GDP8095	0.006	0.016	.0002
LGDP80	3256	5181	2745
EDU	5.0	6.9	4.3
INV	.216	.230	.211
SAVE	.178	.184	.176
RENT	.069	.001	.095
GS	.007	.092	−.026

Our basic cross-country regression is reported in regression (1) in Table 5.2. The dependent variable is the period average of the growth rate of GDP (in PPP) per capita (1980 to 1995). The independent or explanatory variables are the natural log of GDP (in PPP) per capita in 1980 (*LGDP80*), human capital, measured in terms of years of educational attainment in 1980 (of population over 25) (*EDU*) (from Barro and Lee, 1993) and the investment ratio in 1980 (*INV80*) and period average of the share of resource rents in GDP (*RENT*). The following dummy variables are included to control for regional factors (see Appendix 5.1 for further details): Sub-Saharan Africa (*SSA*); Central America (*CAM*); Latin America (*LAAM*); Middle East and North Africa (*MENA*); and East Asia (*EASIA*).

The negative coefficient on initial income (*LGDP80*) implies a rate of conditional convergence of about 1 per cent per year (that is, 0.9 per cent). Both educational attainment and investment variables have the expected positive signs although each is significant only at the 10 per cent level. Turning now to the question of the resource curse, the coefficient on our variable indicating resource abundance, *RENT*, is both negative and significant (at the 5 per cent level). A 10 per cent increase in the share of resource rents in GDP regression is estimated to decrease the growth rate of per capita GDP by about 0.5 per cent. Hence, the negative relationship between resource abundance and growth is, on the basis of this evidence, non-trivial. The magnitude of the relationship is also comparable to that found in, for example, Sachs and Warner (1997), although any such comparison needs to be made with care. For example, Sachs and Warner propose a different indicator of resource abundance, the share of primary product exports in GDP.[8] This differs from *RENT* in two regards: firstly, it is broader than *RENT* in that it includes, for example, agricultural primary exports;

secondly, it is arguably not such a direct measure of resource depletion in that it does not measure resource rents. However, the two indicators would be expected to be relatively highly correlated in practice.

Table 5.2   Resource abundance and economic growth

	(1)
LGDP80	$-.0086^{***}$
	$(.0031)$
EDU	$.0017^{*}$
	$(.0009)$
INV80	$.0514^{*}$
	$(.0271)$
RENT	$-.0502^{**}$
	$(.0188)$
SSA	$-.0268^{***}$
	$(.0060)$
CAM	$-.0162^{***}$
	$(.0041)$
LAAM	$-.0098^{**}$
	$(.0047)$
MENA	$-.0093^{*}$
	$(.0053)$
E. ASIA	$.0256^{**}$
	$(.0100)$
C	$.0676^{***}$
	$(.0195)$
R^2	0.59
N	91

Notes:
Standard errors in parentheses.
Standard errors are corrected for heteroskedasticity using White's procedure.
***   significant at the 1% level.
**   significant at the 5% level.
*   significant at the 10% level.

To the extent that support for the resource curse hypothesis can be found, the interesting issue is how this curse arises. McMahon (1997) posits a number of mechanisms whereby resource abundance allows governments either to implement undesirable policies or to prolong the duration of existing inefficient (that is, growth-dampening) policies. Similarly, Lane and Tornell (1996) argue that the larger the windfall the greater the incentive of weak government to yield to the demands of powerful rent-seeking groups. One way of quantifying the impact of policy in explaining the resource curse is by interacting policy variables with our variable of resource abundance. For example, interacting our variable *RENT* with various policy-related parameters – such as the share of government expenditure in GDP – might indicate whether it is the combination of resource abundance and government size or particular components of government spending that 'explains' the resource curse.

Table 5.3 summarizes the results of growth regressions that seek to investigate a possible role for government policy in the context of the resource curse. Table 5.3 introduces three policy-related variables: (i) the share of government investment in GDP (*GINV*); (ii) the share of government consumption in GDP (*GCON*); and, (iii) the share of public sector wages and salaries in (total) government expenditure (*WAGE*).

While we did not find the combination of resource abundance and (total) government expenditure to be a significant determinant of the resource curse (not reported here), Table 5.3 indicates some interesting findings for the components of public spending; that is, government investment and consumption. Regressions (1) and (2) examine the role of government investment. We might speculate that government investment could have either a positive or negative relationship with growth. On the one hand, public investment might be interpreted as a relatively productive use of economic resources. On the other hand, McMahon (1997) describes various unproductive public investment booms in resource-rich countries, especially in the construction sector. Regression (1) includes *GINV* as an explanatory variable and finds that coefficient on this variable is negative but insignificant. In regression (2) the interaction between *GINV* and *RENT* is introduced. It is important to note that the coefficient on the interaction $RENT^*GINV$ has no direct interpretation in terms of the magnitude of its impact on the per capita GDP growth rate. However, a positive (or negative) coefficient would indicate whether resource-abundant countries engaging in higher levels of public investment have enjoyed a higher (or lower) growth rate than those resource-abundant countries that have not followed this course of action. Interestingly, in regression (2), the coefficient on this variable is positive and is also significant, although only at the 10 per cent level. The coefficient on *RENT* remains negative and highly significant. It should be noted, however, that the finding for $RENT^*GINV$ also (tentatively) suggests somewhat less intuitively that public investment makes a greater contribution to economic growth in resource-abundant countries.

Turning to the impact of government consumption in the context of resource abundance, regression (4) indicates that those countries that are

Table 5.3   Government expenditure and the resource curse

	(1)	(2)	(3)	(4)	(5)	(6)
LGDP80	−.0057*	−.0064*	−.0073	−.0058*	−.0037	−.0034
	(.0035)	(.0035)	(.0035)	(.0034)	(.0036)	(.0034)
EDU	.0011	.0010	.0008	.0003	.0002	.0007
	(0010)	(.0010)	(0011)	(.0011)	(0013)	(.0013)
INV80	.0376	.0386	.0479	.0223	.0154	.0437
	(.0309)	(.0293)	(.0312)	(.0341)	(.0289)	(.0277)
RENT	−.0379*	−.0824***	−.0533**	.0306	−.0494**	.1172*
	(.0217)	(.0243)	(.0214)	(.0363)	(.0204)	(.0651)
GINV	−.0232	−.1017				
	(.0734)	(.0948)				
RENT*GINV		.6783*				
		(.3696)				
GCON			−.0218	.0634		
			(.0386)	(.0417)		
RENT*GCON				−.4702***		
				(.1496)		
WAGE					−.0035	.0458
					(.0219)	(.0321)
RENT*WAGE						−.6280***
						(.2207)
SSA	−.0270***	−.0283***	−.0301***	−.0308***	−.0299***	−.0320***
	(.0071)	(.0073)	(.0063)	(.0064)	(.0073)	(.0072)
CAM	−.0160***	−.0159***	−.0142***	−.0137***	−.0130***	−.0189***
	(.0044)	(.0045)	(.0037)	(.0035)	(.0035)	(.0042)
LAAM	−.0113**	−.0108**	−.0085	−.0096*	−.0122**	−.0125***
	(.0053)	(.0055)	(.0057)	(.0055)	(.0048)	(.0047)
MENA	−.0061	−.0050	−.0108*	−.0094*	−.0066	−.0050
	(.0057)	(.0057)	(.0059)	(.0063)	(.0055)	(.0055)
E. ASIA	.0232*	.0229**	.0261**	.0282***	.0242**	.0188
	(.0121)	(.0121)	(.0103)	(.0119)	(.0113)	(.0119)
C	.0510**	.0605**	.0608***	.0469**	.0460*	.0238
	(.0247)	(.0261)	(.0217)	(.0211)	(.0254)	(.0273)
R^2	0.52	0.53	0.61	0.63	0.54	0.58
N	83	83	79	79	76	76

Notes:
Standard errors in parentheses.
Standard errors are corrected for heteroskedasticity using White's procedure.
*** significant at the 1% level.
** significant at the 5% level.
* significant at the 10% level.

resource rich and where government consumption is relatively high have experienced, on average, lower economic growth. In addition, the coefficient on *RENT* is now positive but insignificant. This seems to be an interesting result. It suggests that *current* government expenditure items could explain much of the resource curse. To explore this further, we introduce an additional variable reflecting a specific item of government consumption; namely, wages and salaries of government employees. McMahon (1997) suggests that a higher share of the public wage-bill in government expenditure might be indicative of the success of rent-seeking in the public sector and that resource abundance makes it 'easier' for governments to acquiesce to the demands of its employees. Regression (6) shows that the coefficient on the interaction of *WAGE* and *RENT* is negative and highly significant. In addition, the coefficient on *RENT* is now positive and significant although only at the 10 per cent level.

To summarize these findings, it would appear that there is weak evidence to suggest that governments that have used resource abundance to finance investment have fared better in terms of enjoying the economic benefits of that windfall.[9] However, there is stronger evidence to support the contrary proposition that those countries that have primarily used resource abundance to finance current consumption have fared far less well. Hence, our findings show that it is the interaction of government consumption and resources that provides an explanation of the curse.[10] Furthermore, once we control for this interaction, it would appear that the impact of resource abundance on economic growth becomes insignificant (regression (4)) or tentatively positive (regression (6)). Given our focus on sustainability, such results are reassuring in that it appears that one way that the curse might be averted is by avoiding the dissipation of resource rents in current consumption. Indeed, this is the essence of much of the current interest in genuine saving and it is to this to which we now turn.

One preliminary question, in this regard, is the extent to which focusing on the genuine savings rate provides new information on the accumulation of wealth. Genuine saving measures the extent to which countries are, on balance, liquidating or creating national wealth. In other words, observation of the genuine savings rate contains useful information regarding the extent to which the proceeds of resource depletion have been used to finance investment (rather than current consumption), whereas conventional investment and saving ratios measure only gross accumulation. Of course, it could be the case that either gross savings or investment would be an adequate proxy for genuine saving. That is, genuine savings could be highly correlated with conventional measures of wealth accumulation. Table 5.4 therefore reports simple correlations between period average savings, investment and genuine saving. While all of these pairwise correlations are highly significant (that is, at the 1 per cent level) the correlation between genuine savings and savings is slightly less than 25 per cent. There is a stronger correlation between investment and genuine saving (45 per cent) but even here it would still appear that genuine saving potentially may provide new and additional information about wealth accumulation.

Table 5.4 Pairwise relationships between savings and investment rates

	GS	*SAVE*	*INV*
GS	1.000		
SAVE	0.249	1.000	
INV	0.446	0.690	1.000

Table 5.5 evaluates whether genuine saving offers anything in terms of understanding the determinants of economic growth. In other words, have countries with higher rates of genuine saving enjoyed, on average, higher growth rates? In particular, are resource-abundant countries with low or negative genuine saving more likely to have experienced the resource curse? Regression (1) in Table 5.5 indicates that there is a positive and significant correlation between initial period genuine saving (*GS80*) and the growth rate of GDP per capita. A 10 per cent increase in the genuine savings ratio is associated with a 0.3 per cent increase in the growth rate of GDP per capita. That is, countries with lower genuine savings rates experienced, on average and other things being equal, lower economic growth. This result holds even if *INV80* is included as an explanatory variable.

Regression (2) offers evidence regarding the relationship between resource abundance, saving and growth. It does so by examining the impact of resource abundance on growth according to whether countries have experienced low or negative genuine saving. One simple prediction would be that, to the extent that savings are used productively, those countries that avoided low or negative genuine savings are more likely to have avoided the resource curse. In order to test this proposition, we introduce two variables reflecting resource abundance. The first, *RENT(GS≤0)*, takes a value equal to the period average share of rents in GDP (*RENT*) if period average genuine saving (*GS*) is zero or negative and a value of zero otherwise. The second, *RENT*(GS>0), takes a value equal to *RENT* if *GS* is greater than zero and a value of zero otherwise. Regression (2) does strongly suggest that those resource-abundant countries that experienced zero or negative genuine savings were characterized by the resource curse. That is, the coefficient on *RENT*(GS≤0) is negative and significant at the 1 per cent level. The coefficient on *RENT(GS>0)* is also negative but is not significant; for example, countries that avoided zero or negative zero savings do not seem, on average, to have experienced the resource curse.

Table 5.5   Genuine savings and growth

	(1)	(2)
LGDP80	−.0089***	−.0082***
	(.0031)	(.0028)
EDU	.0019*	.0016
	(.0010)	(.0010)
INV80		.0535*
		(.0276)
GS80	.0338**	
	(.0156)	
RENT(GS≤0)		−.0528***
		(.0186)
RENT(GS>0)		−.0122
		(.0486)
SSA	−.0251***	−.0264***
	(.0061)	(.0060)
CAM	−.0159***	−.0155***
	(.0041)	(.0040)
LAAM	−.0095**	−.0097**
	(.0045)	(.0040)
MENA	−.0094*	.0092*
	(.0052)	(.0055)
E. ASIA	.0273***	.0227**
	(.0098)	(.0101)
C	.0772***	.0633***
	(.0200)	(.0192)
R^2	0.58	0.60
N	91	91

Notes:
Standard errors in parentheses.
Standard errors are corrected for heteroskedasticity using White's procedure.
*** significant at the 1% level.
** significant at the 5% level.
* significant at the 10% level.

It would also be useful to examine the extent to which resource abundance has led, other things being equal, to an increased savings response in resource abundant countries. Table 5.6 provides a summary of regression results which use as the dependent variable either the period average gross savings ratio (*SAVE*) or period average gross investment ratio (*INV*). The results reported here suggest that while few consistent findings emerge from examining determinants of savings *or* investments in isolation, a number of interesting insights arguably emerge from examining both indicators of wealth accumulation concurrently.

Table 5.6   Saving, investment and resource abundance

	Dependent variable Gross saving (SAVE)			Dependent variable Gross investment (INV)		
	(1)	(2)	(3)	(4)	(5)	(6)
LGDP80	.0606***	.0523***	.0477***	.0112	.0102	.0098
	(.0088)	(.0129)	(.0119)	(.0071)	(.0081)	(.0081)
RENT	.7362***	.5420*	.0349	.2037	.1330	−.4493
	(.1912)*	(.2719)	(.3722)	(.1845)	(.2545)	(.3913)
(RENT)²	−1.0855**	−.1829	2.3538*	−.3264	.1523	2.6383*
	(.5300)	(1.0530)	(1.3949)	(.5040)	(.9360)	(1.4346)
DICRGE		.0140	.0145		.0166	−.0019
		(.0234)	(.0308)		(.0164)	(.0239)
RENT* DICRGE			.9023*			1.1143**
			(.5139)			(.4843)
(RENT)² *DICRGE			−4.9851*			−4.984***
			(1.7818)			(1.6792)
SSA	−.0026	.0112	−.0030	−.0161	−.0156	−.0269
	(.0233)	(.0248)	(.0235)	(.0162)	(.0179)	(.0167)
CAM	−.0039	−.0043	.0107	.0202	.0147	.0220
	(.0202)	(.0251)	(.0234)	(.0206)	(.0247)	(.0210)
LAAM	−.0073	−.0015	.0107	−.0423**	−.0341	−.0270
	(.0196)	(.0225)	(.0186)	(.0205)	(.0213)	(.0203)
MENA	−.0047	−.0068	−.0070	.0240	.0336	.0368
	(.0271)	(.0322)	(0.0315)	(.0190)	(.0255)	(.0245)
E. ASIA	.1655***	.1629***	.1594***	.1060***	.1074***	.1058***
	(.0270)	(.0278)	(0.0268)	(.0211)	(.0210)	(.0208)
C	−.3585***	−.2955***	−.2543***	.1125*	.1081	.1246*
	(.0793)	(.1042)	(0.0935)	(.0639)	(.0675)	(.0646)
R²	0.683	0.664	0.711	0.378	0.475	0.543
N	87	73	73	88	73	73

Notes:
Standard errors in parentheses.
Standard errors are corrected for heteroskedasticity using White's procedure.
*** significant at the 1% level.
** significant at the 5% level.
* significant at the 10% level.

Firstly, resource abundance, as measured by the period average resource rent share (*RENT*), appears to lead to a highly positive (and significant) savings effort in regression (1). This regression also includes as an explanatory variable the square of *RENT* ($RENT^2$) which is negative and highly significant. This would appear to indicate that the greater its resource abundance the greater the difficulty that country has, on average, in transforming the liquidation of this natural wealth into a correspondingly higher savings rate; that is, resource-abundant countries save more but at a declining rate. However, the corresponding regression for the determinants of investment (regression (4)) appears to yield no similar insights, which is perhaps surprising.

Secondly, Sachs and Warner (1999) and Stijns (2000) draw attention to the importance of the existence of good quality institutions in enabling countries to realize the benefits of resource abundance. It would also be interesting to see if institutional quality has any implications for sustainability and the transformation of resource abundance into additional saving and investment. In an earlier contribution, Sachs and Warner (1997) proposed an index of institutional quality (ICRGE) as a candidate determinant of cross-country growth differences. This is an average of indices of rule of law, bureaucratic quality, government corruption, investment expropriation risk and contract repudiation risk.[11] This index takes a possible value between 1 and 10 where higher index values correspond to higher quality of institutions. Regressions (2) and (4) introduce *DICRGE*, which is a dummy variable taking a value of 1 if a country has greater than the median score for Sachs and Warner's index of institutional quality and a value of zero otherwise. However, for both savings and investment regressions this variable does not seem to be a significant determinant of accumulation, although this finding can largely be explained by the correlation of institutional quality with initial income (*LGDP80*).[12]

Thirdly, the combination of both resource abundance and institutional quality in explaining gross saving and investment is examined in regressions (3) and (6) in Table 5.6. One expectation might be that it is the presence of higher quality institutions in the context of resource abundance that might lead to a more favourable savings and investment response. For savings determinants (regression (3)), we find a tentative relationship in the interaction of resource abundance and institutional quality ($RENT^*DICRGE$) is positive but significant only at the 10 per cent level. For investment, however, this finding is somewhat stronger in that in regression (6) the coefficient on $RENT^*DICRGE$ is significant at the 5 per cent level. Thus, taken together this appears to suggest evidence that resource-dependent countries with relatively good quality institutions appear to be better placed to transform the liquidation of resource wealth into additional genuine saving. However, it should also be noted that in both regressions (3) and (6) the coefficients on the interaction of the square of *RENT* and institutional quality ($RENT^{2*}DICRGE$) are negative and (highly) significant. This seems to indicate that to the extent that the combination of resource abundance and institutional quality leads, other things being equal, to a greater savings or investment effort it does so at a declining rate. Put another way, highly resource-dependent countries with relatively good quality institutions appear to find it more difficult to transform the liquidation of resource wealth into additional saving or investment.

CONCLUSIONS

Resource abundance should, in principle, confer an economic advantage on resource-owning countries. However, various studies have found that, in practice, these benefits have not been realized. This is the so-called 'resource curse hypothesis' or 'paradox of plenty'; the finding that resource abundance can lead to negative development and economic growth outcomes. In this chapter, we confirm this result by demonstrating that our main indicator of resource abundance, the share of resource rents in GDP, is negatively correlated with the GDP per capita growth rate.

We find some evidence to support the view that the outward manifestation of resource mismanagement might be the use of resource revenues to finance government expenditure. Hence, we present tentative evidence that governments in resource-abundant countries that have financed public investment using resource revenues have avoided the resource curse. There is stronger evidence that those governments in resource-abundant countries that have consumed the proceeds of this abundance are those that, on average, have experienced a significant resource curse. This was found for the relationship between resource depletion and government consumption, in general, and spending on public wages and salaries in particular.

Regarding the wider relationship between the resource curse, savings and growth, we find that those resource-abundant countries that have suffered from a curse appear to be those countries that have low or negative genuine savings. The savings and investment response that might be expected to arise in the presence of resource abundance will also depend on a number of factors, including the quality of institutions, that have a bearing on the efficiency of investments and risk to economic resources invested for the future. In this respect, we have found that there is some evidence to suggest that resource-abundant countries with good quality institutions have enjoyed greater rates of investment and, to a lesser extent, saving. It would be interesting in future work to examine the determinants of the genuine saving rate. These results, we argue, offer another perspective on the resource curse hypothesis: countries where growth has lagged behind the average are those where the *combination* of natural resource, macroeconomic and public expenditure policies has led to a low rate of (genuine) saving.

NOTES

1. This chapter is based on Atkinson and Hamilton (2003).
2. To the extent that population in this economy is not constant a more satisfactory indicator of sustainability is the change in (total) wealth per capita – see Chapter 3.
3. Barbier (1999) has also examined the links between resource abundance and availability on innovation within an endogenous growth framework.
4. This follows the sampling approach taken in studies such as Sachs and Warner (1995) rather than studies such as Davis (1995) which focuses exclusively on countries which are characterized as resource – (for example, mineral) rich. In practice, the inclusion does not affect the major conclusions outlined in this chapter.
5. Note that for timber resources it is only that portion of timber harvest that exceeds the natural growth of the forest that is valued.
6. The inclusion of the net timber accumulation, however, does not appear to markedly change the findings outlined in this chapter.
7. Data based on average costs will overestimate rents if marginal costs are increasing in extraction.
8. In addition, Sachs and Warner (for example, 1997) examine a different (but overlapping) time period and estimate a somewhat different model than that in Table 5.2 here.
9. However, while the findings here with respect to the resource curse yield some statistically significant explanations, it is apparent that the results for other variables that we would expect to have a bearing on economic growth, such as initial investment and human capital, are somewhat weaker. A similar 'anomaly' is found by Lane and Torrell (1996) for (largely) insignificant results for initial income and human capital as growth determinants but highly significant results for their variables of interest (that is, rent-seeking behaviour and terms of trade windfalls). This is attributed to multicollinearity and the absence from their model of other variables that might more comprehensively account for growth determinants as in studies such as Barro and Sala-i-Martin (1995).
10. A caveat to this specific finding is that few studies using cross-country regressions have identified a robust relationship of any particular policy variable with growth (Temple, 1999). Hence, it could be that significant variables are better interpreted as proxies for policy in general, rather than supporting any specific mechanism.
11. Sachs and Warner (1997) developed this index, in turn, from data by Political Risk Services.
12. A regression (not reported in this chapter) of the determinants of per capita GDP growth that included *DICRGE* indicated that while higher institutional quality was a significant determinant of higher growth the interaction of *DICRGE* with *RENT* did not appear to provide an additional (direct) explanation of the resource curse.

APPENDIX 5A.1   COUNTRIES IN SAMPLE

Central America
Barbados
Dominican Rep.
Grenada
Haiti
Jamaica
Trinidad and Tobago
Belize
Costa Rica
El Salvador
Guatemala

Latin America
Mexico
Argentina
Bolivia
Brazil
Chile
Colombia
Ecuador
Paraguay
Peru
Suriname
Uruguay
Venezuela

Middle East and North Africa
Bahrain
Iran
Israel
Saudi Arabia
Syria
Algeria
Egypt
Morocco
Tunisia

East Asia
Hong Kong
Indonesia
Korea, Rep.
Malaysia
Philippines
Singapore
Thailand

Other Asia
China
Myanmar
Papua New Guinea
Bangladesh
India
Nepal
Pakistan
Sri Lanka

OECD (high income)
Australia
Austria
Belgium
Canada
Denmark
Finland
France
Germany
Ireland
Italy
Japan
Luxembourg
Netherlands
New Zealand
Norway
Portugal
Spain
Sweden
Switzerland
United Kingdom
United States

Other Europe
Greece
Turkey

Sub-Saharan Africa
Benin
Burkina Faso
Burundi
Cameroon
Central African Republic
Chad
Congo
Cote d'Ivoire
Gabon
Gambia, the
Ghana
Guinea-Bissau
Kenya
Madagascar
Malawi
Mali
Mauritania
Mauritius
Namibia
Niger
Nigeria
Rwanda
Senegal
Sierra Leone
South Africa
Togo
Uganda
Zambia
Zimbabwe

APPENDIX 5A.2   LIST OF VARIABLES

GDP8095   rate of growth of GDP per capita (in purchasing power parity) 1980 to 1995

LGDP80   log of GDP per capita (in purchasing power parity) in 1980

EDU   educational attainment (mean years of education) in 1980

INV80   investment ratio in 1980

INV   investment ratio (average 1980 to 1995)

SAVE80   savings ratio in 1980

SAVE   savings ratio (average 1980 to 1995)

GS80   genuine savings ratio in 1980

GS   genuine savings ratio (average 1980 to 1995)

RENT   share of resource rents in GDP (average 1980 to 1995)

SXP   share of primary product exports in GDP (average 1980 to 1995)

SSA   dummy variable for Sub-Saharan Africa

CAM   dummy variable for Central America

LAAM   dummy variable for Latin America

EASIA   dummy variable for East Asia

MENA   dummy variable for Middle East and North Africa

GEXP   share of government expenditure in GDP (average 1980 to 1995)

GINV   share of government investment in GDP (average 1980 to 1995)

GCON   share of government consumption in GDP (average 1980 to 1995)

WAGE   share of public wages and salaries in government expenditure (average 1980 to 1995)

DICRGE   dummy variable based on Sachs and Warner's (1997) index of institutional quality, which equals 1 if a country has an above median score for this index and 0 otherwise.

6.   A Hartwick Rule counterfactual

INTRODUCTION[1]

As presented in Chapter 5, there is by now a substantial empirical literature documenting the 'resource curse' or 'paradox of plenty'. Resource-rich countries should enjoy an advantage in the development process, and yet these countries experienced lower GDP growth rates post-1970 than less well endowed countries. A number of plausible explanations for this phenomenon have been suggested: inflated currencies may impede the development of the non-oil export sector ('Dutch disease'); easy money in the form of resource rents may reduce incentives to implement needed economic reforms; and volatile resource prices may complicate macroeconomic management, exacerbating political conflicts over the sharing and management of resource revenues.

In the most extreme examples, levels of welfare in resource-rich countries are lower today than they were in 1970 – development has not been sustained by Pezzey's (1989) definition. The Hartwick Rule (Hartwick, 1977) offers what Solow (1986) termed a 'rule of thumb' for sustainability in exhaustible resource economies – a maximal constant level of consumption can be sustained if the value of investment equals the value of rents on extracted resources at each point in time. For countries dependent on such wasting assets this rule offers a prescription for sustainable development,[2] a prescription that Botswana in particular has followed with its diamond wealth (Lange and Wright, 2004).

Drawing on a 30-year time series of resource rent data underlying the *World Development Indicators* (World Bank, 2004), in this chapter we construct a 'Hartwick Rule counterfactual': how rich would countries be in the year 2000 if they had followed the Hartwick Rule since 1970? The results are, in many cases, striking.

Our empirical work draws upon new results[3] showing that the Hartwick Rule is a special case of a more general rule for sustainability. We extend the results in Hamilton and Withagen (forthcoming) to determine the properties of a constant net saving rule – constant positive net saving entails a path for consumption that rises without bound. We then apply this rule and the standard Hartwick Rule to our historical data on investment and resource rents covering 1970–2000.

THE GENERALIZED RULE FOR SUSTAINABILITY

For a quite general model of a dynamic economy, Hamilton and Withagen (forthcoming) establish that if the economy is competitive (households maximize utility while firms maximize profits) and if externalities are internalized through Pigouvian taxes, then utility U, consumption C, net (genuine) saving G and interest rate r are related as follows:

$$\dot{U} = U_C\left(rG - \dot{G}\right).\tag{6.1}$$

This relates the current change in utility to the sign and rate of growth of genuine saving. But, since optimality is not assumed, it also provides the basis for a general rule for sustainability (non-declining utility).[4] If the policy rule is to hold $G = 0$ for all time, then this is just the standard Hartwick Rule, yielding constant utility. If $G > 0$ and $\dot{G}/G < r$ for all time, then utility is everywhere increasing.[5]

For our purposes we assume a simple economy with an exhaustible resource that is essential for production, as in Dasgupta and Heal (1979). For capital K and resource extraction R, the production function is Cobb-Douglas, $F = K^\alpha R^\beta$, $\alpha + \beta = 1$. Output is divided between consumption and investment, so that $F(K, R) = C + \dot{K}$. Utility is given by $U = U(C)$. Resource extraction is assumed to be efficient, implying that $S_0 = \int_0^\infty R ds$ – the initial resource stock S_0 is exhausted over the infinite time horizon. The initial endowment of produced capital is K_0.

Competitiveness in the Dasgupta–Heal economy implies that the resource price is equal to F_R, that the interest rate is F_K, and that the Hotelling Rule is satisfied,

$$\dot{F}_R\big/F_R = F_K.\tag{6.2}$$

Genuine saving is given by,

$$G \equiv \dot{K} - F_R R.\tag{6.3}$$

Hamilton and Hartwick (2005) establish the following basic proposition for the Dasgupta-Heal economy, analogous to expression (6.1):

Proposition 6.1: In the competitive Dasgupta–Heal economy, $\dot{C} = F_K G - \dot{G}$.

Hamilton and Hartwick also prove the following wealth accounting result. It will be useful in proving the main proposition below.

Proposition 6.2: Under constant returns to scale total wealth is given by:

$$W = K + F_R S = \int_t^\infty Ce^{-\int_t^s F_K d\tau} ds.$$

The following proposition characterizes a particular instance of a generalized sustainability rule in the Dasgupta–Heal economy, an instance we will exploit empirically in the next section.

Proposition 6.3: If $\alpha > \beta$ then $G = \bar{G} > 0$ $\forall t$ for constant $\bar{G} < \alpha F(0)$ is a feasible program for rising consumption. Initial consumption will be lower than on the Hartwick Rule ($\bar{G} = 0$) path, but consumption increases without bound. Wealth on this path is greater than under the standard Hartwick Rule, and maximum wealth is independent of the initial resource stock S_0.

Proof: See Appendix 6A.1

Having established the properties of this specific sustainability rule for the Dasgupta–Heal economy, we now turn to the empirical application of the rule to historical data.

HYPOTHETICAL ESTIMATES OF CAPITAL STOCKS

While the foregoing theory can be shown to apply to rules for *saving* in an open economy, we will limit ourselves to *investment* rules in the empirical application. All of the countries which are highlighted in the empirical results had significant net foreign debts in 2000. Rather than looking at the more complex question of whether resource rents could have been used to either pay down foreign debt or invest in domestic assets, we limit ourselves to comparing an estimate of the current stock of produced capital with a hypothetical estimate of how large this stock could be if resource rents had been invested in produced capital. We assume that all resource rents are invested in produced capital for simplicity, although the theory suggests more generally that resource rents could be invested in a range of assets, including human capital. If any of the countries highlighted below had in fact been investing their resource rents in human capital (quite unlikely given the observed levels of per capita income) then our methodology would produce a biased picture of their investment performance.

In order to examine a variety of counterfactuals, we derive four estimates of produced capital stock using empirical data covering 1970–2000: (i) a baseline capital stock derived from investment series and a perpetual inventory model (PIM); (ii) a capital stock derived from strict application of the standard Hartwick Rule; (iii) a capital stock derived from the constant net or genuine investment rule; and (iv) a capital stock derived from the maximum of observed net investment and the investment required under the constant genuine investment rule. All investment and resource rent series are measured in constant 1995 US dollars at nominal exchange rates.

Details of the PIM are given in Chapter 3. For each country the estimate of baseline capital stock is given by,

$$K_t = \sum_{s=0}^{T-1} I_{t-s} \left(1 - \gamma\right)^s.$$

Here I is gross investment, the average asset service life T is assumed to be 20 years and the depreciation rate γ is 5 per cent – these are held constant across countries and over time. We use the year 2000 as our basis for comparison of capital stocks.

For genuine investment I^G, net investment N, depreciation of produced capital D and resource depletion R we have the following basic identities at any point in time:

$$I^G \equiv I - D - R$$

$$N \equiv I - D = I^G + R.$$

Note that, given a base-year capital stock estimate, it is possible to estimate capital stocks beyond the base year by simply accumulating net investment in each period. Therefore, for constant $\bar{I}^G$, we estimate the counterfactual series of produced capital for each country as:

$$K_{2000}^* = K_{1970} + \sum_{i=1971}^{2000} \left(\bar{I}^G + R_i\right)$$

$$K_{2000}^{**} = K_{1970} + \sum_{i=1971}^{2000} \max\left(N_i, \bar{I}^G + R_i\right).$$

We calculate two versions of K^* in what follows – one with $\bar{I}^G = 0$ (the standard Hartwick rule), and a second with $\bar{I}^G$ equal to a constant 5 per cent of 1987 GDP. The choice of a particular level of genuine investment for the analysis is obviously arbitrary. We use 5 per cent of 1987 GDP for the following reasons: (i) there is some logic to choosing the mid-point of our time series of data from 1970–2000, but 1987 is a slightly better choice, falling after the early 1980s' recession, after the collapse of oil prices in 1986, and before the early 1990s' recession; and (ii) a 5 per cent genuine investment rate is roughly the average achieved by low income countries over time. Since the elasticity of output with respect to produced capital α is implicitly greater than 0.5 in the theoretical model of the preceding section, the choice of 5 per cent of GDP ensures that the feasibility condition $\bar{G} <$ $\alpha F(0)$ of Proposition 6.3 is satisfied.

Resource depletion is estimated as the sum of total rents on the extraction of the following commodities: crude oil, natural gas, coal, bauxite, copper, gold, iron, lead, nickel, phosphate, silver and zinc. While the underlying theory suggests that scarcity rents are what should be invested under the Hartwick Rule (that is, price minus marginal extraction cost), the World Bank data do not include information on marginal extraction costs. The implication of this in the current case is that it gives an upward bias to the hypothetical capital stock estimates under the genuine investment rules.

There is another clear divergence between our empirical methods and the theory of the preceding section. In the autarkic Dasgupta–Heal economy presented above, the choice of policy rule also determines the level and path of resource rents (F_R). By using historical rents in our calculations we are clearly diverging from the theory. However, in most instances we would expect resource exporters to be price takers, which favours using historical rents. If resource prices change exogenously, a further adjustment to saving to reflect future capital gains is required (see Vincent et al., 1997), but Chapter 9 will show that the adjustment is typically small if historical price trends are extrapolated.

When comparing estimates of the stock of produced capital for different countries, it is worth noting that the PIM underestimates the capital stock for countries with very old infrastructure, as in most European countries. The value of roads, bridges and buildings constructed many decades and even centuries ago is not captured by the PIM. Pritchett (2000) makes a different point, that low returns on investments imply that the PIM overestimates the value of capital in developing countries. Our methodology assumes that both the PIM and cumulated net investments are in fact adding up productive investments. To the extent that this is not the case, our estimated capital stock levels should be lower in developing countries – but we are primarily interested in relative stock levels, which makes the point less salient.

EMPIRICAL RESULTS

How rich would countries be in the year 2000 had they followed the Hartwick Rule since 1970? Based on the preceding methodology, Table 6A.1

in Appendix 6A.2, presents the year 2000 produced capital stock and the changes in this stock which would result from the alternative investment rules. The countries shown in this table are those having both exhaustible resources and a sufficiently long time series of data on gross investment and resource rents. For reference, the table also shows the average share of resource rents in GDP over 1970–2000. Note that negative entries in this table imply that countries actually invested more than the policy rule suggests.

For the standard Hartwick Rule, Figure 6.1 scatters resource abundance, expressed as the average share of exhaustible resource rents in GDP, against the percentage difference between actual capital accumulation and counterfactual capital accumulation. Using 5 per cent of GDP as the threshold for high resource dependence, Figure 6.1 divides countries into the four groups shown.

The top-right quadrant of the graph displays countries with high resource dependence and a counterfactual capital stock that is higher than the actual (baseline) capital stock. The bottom-left quadrant of the graph displays countries with low natural resource dependence and baseline capital stock that is higher than would be obtained under the Hartwick Rule. These two quadrants include most of the countries in our sample, indicating a high negative correlation between resource abundance and the difference between baseline and counterfactual capital accumulation – a simple regression shows that a 1 per cent increase in resource dependence is associated with a 9 per cent increased difference between counterfactual and actual capital. Clearly the countries in the top-right quadrant have not been following the Hartwick Rule. Economies with very low levels of capital accumulation despite high rents include Nigeria (oil), Venezuela (oil), Trinidad and Tobago (oil and gas), and Zambia (copper); with the exception of Trinidad and Tobago, all of these countries experienced declines in real per capita income over 1970–2000. In the opposite quadrant, economies with low exhaustible resource rent shares but high levels of capital accumulation include Korea, Thailand, Brazil and India. A number of high income countries are also in this group.

Figure 6.1 shows that no country with resource rents higher than 15 per cent of GDP has followed the Hartwick Rule. In many cases the differences are huge. Nigeria, a major oil exporter, could have had a year 2000 stock of produced capital five times higher than the actual stock. Moreover, if these investments had taken place, oil would play a much smaller role in the Nigerian economy today, with likely beneficial impacts on policies affecting other sectors of the economy.[6] Venezuela could have four times as much produced capital. In per capita terms, the economies of Venezuela, Trinidad and Tobago and Gabon, all rich in petroleum, could today have a stock

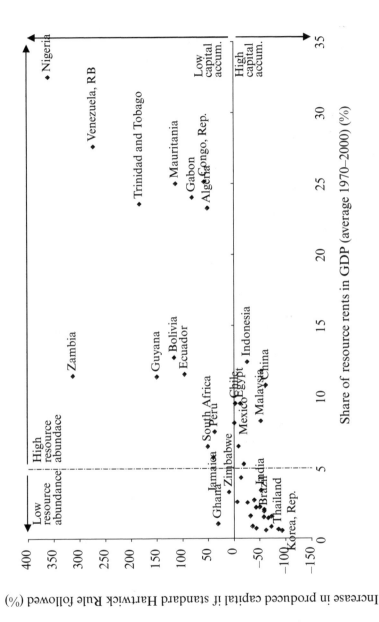

Figure 6.1 Resource abundance and capital accumulation (standard Hartwick Rule)

of produced capital of roughly $30 000 per person, comparable to South Korea (see Figure 6.2).

Consumption rather than investment of resource rents is common in resource-rich countries, but there are exceptions to the trend. In the bottom-right quadrant of Figure 6.1 are high resource-dependent countries which have invested more than the level of exhaustible resource rents. Indonesia, China, Egypt and Malaysia stand out in this group, while Chile and Mexico have effectively followed the Hartwick Rule – growth in produced capital is completely offset by resource depletion.

Among the countries with relatively low natural resource dependence and higher counterfactual capital, we find Ghana (gold, bauxite) and Zimbabwe (gold). This is indicative of very low levels of capital accumulation in these economies.

Figure 6.3 highlights countries which have invested more than their resource rents (as shown by the negative entries on the left side of the figure) but have failed to maintain constant genuine investment levels of at least 5 per cent of 1987 GDP (as shown by the entries on the right). Developing countries in this group include Côte d'Ivoire, Madagascar, Cameroon and Argentina. A number of high income countries also appear in the figure. Sweden could have a stock of capital 36 per cent higher if it had maintained constant genuine investment levels at the specified target. The corresponding difference for the UK is 27 per cent, for Norway 25 per cent and for Denmark 22 per cent. The generally low level of genuine investment levels in the Nordic countries is particularly surprising. Are these countries trading off inter-generational equity against intra-generational equity? Further research would be required to clarify this, a question that is beyond the scope of this chapter.

Finally, the next-to-last column in Table A6.1 shows the change in produced assets for countries if they had genuine investments of at least 5 per cent of 1987 GDP. The positive figures indicate that, with the exception of Singapore, all countries experienced at least one year over 1970–2000 where genuine investments were less than the prescribed constant level.

CONCLUSIONS

As suggested in Hamilton and Withagen (forthcoming), applying the standard Hartwick Rule as development policy would be extreme – it implies a commitment to zero net saving for all time. Conversely, the constant genuine saving rule embodies a commitment to building wealth at each point in time. In a risky world this may be a more palatable development policy.

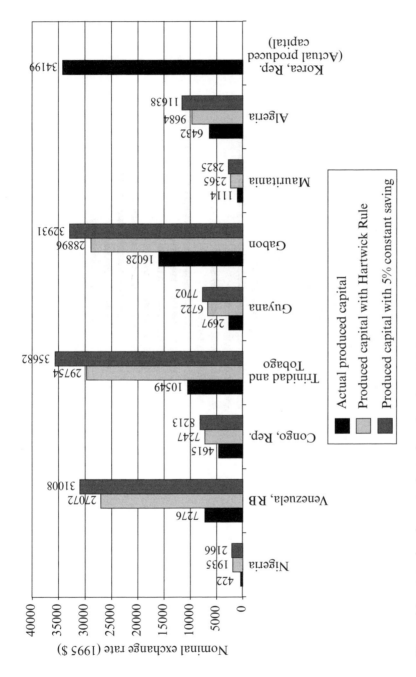

Figure 6.2 Actual and counterfactual produced capital (per capita), 2000

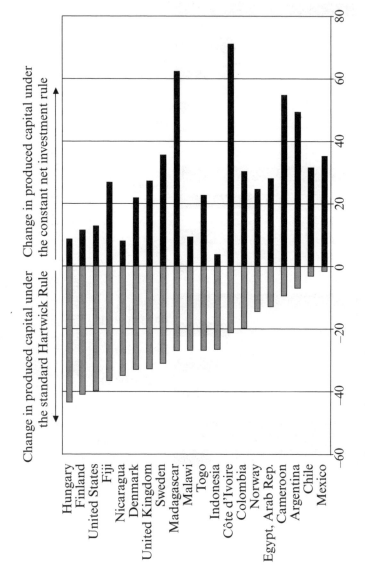

Figure 6.3   Capital accumulation under the Hartwick and constant net investment rules (%)

82

The Hartwick Rule counterfactual calculations show how even a moderate saving effort, equivalent to the average saving effort of the poorest countries in the world, could have substantially increased the wealth of resource-dependent economies. Of course, for the most resource-dependent countries such as Nigeria there is nothing moderate about the implied rate of investment – a Nigerian genuine investment rate of 36.1 per cent of GDP in 1987 is what our calculations suggest under the constant genuine investment rule.

The savings rules presented here are appealing in their simplicity. Maintaining a constant level of genuine saving will yield a development path where consumption grows monotonically, even as exhaustible resource stocks are run down. The real world is more complex. Poor countries place a premium on maintaining consumption levels, with negative effects on saving – the alternative may be starvation. At the same time financial crises, social instability and natural disasters all have deleterious effects on saving. Holding to a simple policy rule in such circumstances would be no small feat.

Saving effort is of course not the whole story in sustaining development. Savings must be channelled into *productive* investments that can underpin future welfare, rather than 'white elephant' projects. As Sarraf and Jiwanji (2001) document, Botswana's successful bid to avoid the resource curse was built upon a whole range of sound macroeconomic and sectoral policies, underpinned by a generally positive political economy. Botswana's absorptive capacity for public investment was a real concern to policymakers, who were prepared to hold resource revenues offshore rather than engage in wasteful investments.

NOTES

1. This chapter is based upon Hamilton et al. (2005).
2. Note that Asheim et al. (2003) question whether the Hartwick Rule is truly prescriptive. This is partly because a commitment to invest resource rents *now* cannot commit future generations to do the same.
3. Hamilton and Hartwick (2005) and Hamilton and Withagen (forthcoming).
4. Note that this is formally the same as expression (2.6) in Chapter 2, but the latter was derived for a PV-optimal economy.
5. Dixit et al. (1980) derive expression (6.1) in the proof of their main proposition, where they show that utility will be constant if either $G = 0 \; \forall t$ or $\dot{G}/G = r \; \forall t, \; G_0 > 0$.
6. We are grateful to Alan Gelb for pointing this out.

APPENDIX 6A.1   PROOF OF PROPOSITION 6.3

Expressions (A6.1)–(A.6.3) establish some basic properties of the path defined by the constant net saving rule:

$$\dot{K} - F_R R = \bar{G} \Rightarrow \ddot{K} = \dot{F}_R R + F_R \dot{R} \tag{6A.1}$$

so that

$$\dot{C} = F_K \dot{K} + F_R \dot{R} - \ddot{K} = F_K \dot{K} - \dot{F}_R R = F_K \bar{G}. \tag{6A.2}$$

Constant returns to scale implies that,

$$C = F - \dot{K} = F_K K + F_R R - \dot{K} = F_K K - \bar{G}. \tag{6A.3}$$

The Hotelling rule is used to derive the following expression for the path of R:

$$\dot{F}_R = F_{RR} \dot{R} + F_{RK} \dot{K} = F_R F_K \quad \Rightarrow \quad \frac{\dot{R}}{R} = -F_K + \frac{\bar{G}}{K}. \tag{6A.4}$$

The growth rates of K and F are derived as follows:

$$\dot{K} = F_R R + \bar{G} = \beta F + \bar{G} \quad \Rightarrow \quad \frac{\dot{K}}{K} = \frac{\beta}{\alpha} F_K + \frac{\bar{G}}{K} \tag{6A.5}$$

$$\frac{\dot{F}}{F} = \alpha \frac{\dot{K}}{K} + \beta \frac{\dot{R}}{R} = \frac{\bar{G}}{K}. \tag{6A.6}$$

Subtracting (6A.5) from (6A.4) we have,

$$\frac{d}{dt}\left(\frac{K}{R}\right) = \frac{1}{\alpha} F_K \frac{K}{R} = \left(\frac{K}{R}\right)^\alpha, \text{ which has a solution,}$$

$$\frac{K}{R} = \left[(1-\alpha)t + \left(K_0/R(0)\right)^{1-\alpha}\right]^{\frac{1}{1-\alpha}}. \tag{6A.7}$$

It will be useful in what follows to derive the integral of the discount factor

$$\int_0^\infty e^{-\int_0^s F_K d\tau}\, ds.$$

We begin by subtracting (6A.5) from (6A.6),

$$\frac{\frac{d}{dt}(F/K)}{F/K} = -\frac{\beta}{\alpha}F_K \quad\Rightarrow\quad e^{-\int_0^t F_K d\tau} = \left(\frac{F}{K}\right)^{\frac{\alpha}{\beta}}\left(\frac{K_0}{F(0)}\right)^{\frac{\alpha}{\beta}}.$$

Since $\left(\dfrac{F}{K}\right)^{\frac{\alpha}{\beta}} = \left(\dfrac{K}{R}\right)^{(\alpha-1)\frac{\alpha}{\beta}}$, (6A.7) implies that

$$e^{-\int_0^t F_K d\tau} = \left(\frac{K_0}{F(0)}\right)^{\frac{\alpha}{\beta}}\left[(1-\alpha)t+\left(K_0/R(0)\right)^{1-\alpha}\right]^{-\frac{\alpha}{\beta}}.\ \text{We can therefore derive,}$$

$$\int_0^\infty e^{-\int_0^s F_K d\tau}\, ds = \frac{\alpha-\beta}{\beta^2}\left(\frac{K_0}{R(0)}\right)^{\beta} = \frac{\alpha(\alpha-\beta)}{\beta^2}\cdot\frac{1}{F_K(0)}. \qquad (6A.8)$$

Expression (6A.4) implies that

$$R = R(0)e^{-\int_0^t F_K - \frac{\bar{G}}{K} d\tau},$$

while (6A.6) implies that

$$F = F(0)e^{\int_0^t \frac{\bar{G}}{K} d\tau}.$$

Now Proposition 2 and expression (E.3) can be used along with the preceding expressions for R and F to derive the following expression for initial wealth:

$$W(0) = K_0 + F_R(0)S_0 = \int_0^\infty Ce^{-\int_0^s F_K d\tau} ds = \int_0^\infty F_K Ke^{-\int_0^s F_K d\tau} ds - \int_0^\infty \bar{G}e^{-\int_0^s F_K d\tau} ds$$

$$= \frac{\alpha F(0)}{R(0)} \int_0^\infty R(0)e^{-\int_0^s F_K - \frac{\bar{G}}{K} d\tau} ds - \frac{\alpha(\alpha - \beta)}{\beta^2} \cdot \frac{1}{F_K(0)} \bar{G}$$

$$= \frac{\alpha F(0)S_0}{R(0)} - \frac{\alpha(\alpha - \beta)}{\beta^2} \cdot \frac{1}{F_K(0)} \bar{G}$$

Since $F_R(0)S_0 = \beta K^\alpha_0 R(0)^{\beta-1} S_0$, this expression can be solved for $R(0)$ to yield,

$$R^{\bar{G}}(0) = (\alpha - \beta)^{\frac{1}{\alpha}} S_0^{\frac{1}{\alpha}} K_0 \left(K_0 + \frac{\alpha(\alpha - \beta)}{\beta^2} \cdot \frac{1}{F_K(0)} \bar{G} \right)^{-\frac{1}{\alpha}}$$

$$= R^H(0)\left(1 + \frac{\alpha - \beta}{\beta^2} \cdot \frac{1}{F(0)} \bar{G} \right)^{-\frac{1}{\alpha}} \tag{6A.9}$$

Here superscript $\bar{G}$ denotes values on the path for the constant savings rule, while superscript H denotes values on the Hartwick Rule ($\bar{G} = 0$) path. (Note that, since $F(0) = F(K_0, R(0))$, we do not have an analytic solution for $R(0)$ in expression (6A.9).) Feasibility (positive initial period resource extraction) requires that $\alpha > \beta$.

Since: $C^{\bar{G}}(0) = F^{\bar{G}}(0) - F_{R^{\bar{G}}}(0)R^{\bar{G}}(0) - \bar{G} = \alpha F^{\bar{G}}(0) - \bar{G}$, it follows (i) that $C^{\bar{G}}(0) < C^H(0)$, and (ii) that $\bar{G} < \alpha F^{\bar{G}}(0)$ is necessary for feasibility (positive initial period consumption). This implies that

$$R^H(0)\left(1 + \frac{\alpha(\alpha - \beta)}{\beta^2} \right)^{-\frac{1}{\alpha}} < R^{\bar{G}}(0) < R^H(0). \tag{6A.10}$$

Initial resource extraction is lower on the constant genuine saving path than on the Hartwick Rule path, and feasibility ensures a strict lower limit for this value.

Expression (6A.9) implies that

$$W^{\bar{G}}(0) = \frac{\alpha}{\alpha - \beta} K_0 + \frac{1}{\beta}\left(\frac{K_0}{R(0)} \right)^\beta \bar{G}. \tag{6A.11}$$

Total wealth is therefore greater under the constant savings rule than under the Hartwick Rule. Note that total wealth is independent of the initial resource endowment S_0 under the Hartwick Rule. Feasibility ($\bar{G} < \alpha F^{\bar{G}}(0)$) implies that,

$$\frac{\alpha}{\alpha - \beta} K_0 < W^{\bar{G}}(0) < \left(\frac{\alpha}{\alpha - \beta} + \frac{\alpha}{\beta} \right) K_0 \text{ or, } W^H(0) < W^{\bar{G}}(0) < W^H(0) + \frac{\alpha}{\beta} K_0.$$

Total wealth under the constant savings rule is therefore constrained by bounds that are independent of initial resource endowment.

Finally, (6A.2) implies that,

$$\dot{C} = F_K \bar{G} = \alpha \left(\frac{K}{R} \right)^{\alpha - 1} \bar{G} = \alpha \left[(1 - \alpha) t + (K_0 / R(0))^{1 - \alpha} \right]^{-1} \bar{G}$$

so that, by integrating and applying expression (6A.3),

$$C = \frac{\alpha}{1 - \alpha} \ln \left[(1 - \alpha)(K_0 / R(0))^{\alpha - 1} t + 1 \right] \bar{G} + \alpha F(0) - \bar{G}. \quad (6A.12)$$

Expression (6A.12) implies that consumption increases without bound under the constant savings rule.

QED

APPENDIX 6A.2

Table 6A.1   Change in produced assets under varying rules for genuine investment (I^G)

	Produced capital in 2000 ($bn 1995 dollars)	$I^G = 0$ (% difference)	$I^G = 5\%$ of 1987 GDP (% difference)	$I^G >= 5\%$ of 1987 GDP (% difference)	Rent/GDP average (1970–2000) (%)
Nigeria	53.5	358.9	413.6	413.6	32.6
Venezuela, RB	175.9	272.1	326.1	326.1	27.7
Congo, Rep.	13.9	57.0	78.0	116.9	25.2
Mauritania	3.0	112.3	153.7	154.0	25.0
Gabon	19.7	80.3	105.5	130.4	24.1
Trinidad and Tobago	13.7	182.1	238.3	239.1	23.6
Algeria	195.4	50.6	80.9	83.9	23.3
Bolivia	13.7	116.1	169.8	177.5	12.8
Indonesia	540.6	−26.5	3.8	32.1	12.5
Ecuador	37.7	95.3	158.0	158.3	11.6
Zambia	7.5	312.3	383.4	388.0	11.5
Guyana	2.1	149.3	185.6	191.2	11.4
China	2899.4	−62.1	−45.0	5.1	10.8
Egypt, Arab Rep.	159.7	−12.9	28.1	36.2	9.5
Chile	151.4	−3.0	31.6	54.0	9.5
Malaysia	305.2	−52.7	−31.4	6.6	8.3

Mexico	975.5	−1.5	35.3	42.2	8.2
Peru	132.3	37.2	98.1	103.9	7.5
Cameroon	24.1	−9.3	54.8	67.6	6.5
South Africa	349.5	50.7	109.3	115.8	6.5
Jamaica	13.4	39.9	87.8	99.6	5.7
Colombia	198.0	−19.7	30.4	39.3	5.3
Norway	456.6	−14.3	24.6	33.0	4.3
India	965.4	−52.9	−18.3	8.6	3.4
Zimbabwe	14.9	9.1	64.8	89.1	3.3
United States	16926.7	−39.8	12.9	26.1	2.7
Argentina	569.6	−6.9	49.4	53.9	2.6
Togo	3.6	−26.8	22.7	55.1	2.6
Pakistan	125.6	−50.7	−1.7	11.1	2.2
Hungary	149.1	−43.5	8.7	22.3	2.2
Morocco	93.8	−59.1	−16.3	7.8	2.0
Brazil	1750.5	−59.0	−6.6	9.1	1.9
United Kingdom	2400.1	−32.7	27.3	32.8	1.6
Dominican Republic	33.8	−73.0	−27.9	1.2	1.6
Philippines	195.0	−58.4	−14.5	10.6	1.5
Honduras	12.3	−66.9	−29.7	8.9	1.5
Ghana	16.1	30.6	73.2	76.7	1.0
Fiji	3.6	−36.5	26.9	59.3	0.9
Benin	4.6	−72.7	−21.7	10.6	0.8
Senegal	10.0	−44.0	14.2	27.5	0.7

Table 6A.1   (continued)

	Produced capital in 2000 ($bn 1995 dollars)	$I^G = 0$ (% difference)	$I^G = 5\%$ of 1987 GDP (% difference)	$I^G >= 5\%$ of 1987 GDP (% difference)	Rent/GDP average (1970–2000) (%)
Thailand	520.6	−86.3	−63.6	3.0	0.7
Haiti	2.8	−62.7	109.2	109.5	0.6
Korea, Rep.	1 607.6	−93.5	−68.6	0.9	0.6
Israel	215.8	−72.8	−31.3	4.2	0.5
Cote d'Ivoire	16.1	−21.2	71.1	108.7	0.5
Bangladesh	89.7	−59.0	−12.9	15.5	0.5
Rwanda	3.9	−83.2	−6.9	24.6	0.4
Sweden	508.0	−31.1	35.6	36.1	0.4
Nicaragua	6.9	−34.9	8.1	44.8	0.3
Spain	1 623.6	−58.9	−15.1	6.1	0.3
Denmark	437.2	−33.0	21.9	28.7	0.2
France	3 724.7	−55.0	−1.9	6.9	0.1
Italy	2 711.2	−44.8	7.5	10.2	0.1
Finland	347.6	−40.9	11.6	23.3	0.1
Belgium	681.9	−48.0	2.3	10.4	0.1
Niger	3.0	9.7	95.2	136.1	0.1
Burundi	1.6	−87.3	10.1	30.2	0.1
Portugal	308.8	−71.0	−30.8	5.7	0.0

Costa Rica	24.1	-80.0	-30.6	3.6	0.0
El Salvador	17.1	-59.7	-2.5	24.6	0.0
Hong Kong, China	445.9	-88.6	-56.4	0.9	0.0
Kenya	20.1	-51.9	2.0	20.8	0.0
Madagascar	4.9	-26.9	62.4	65.5	0.0
Sri Lanka	41.2	-88.1	-55.4	1.0	0.0
Malawi	4.6	-26.8	9.4	68.2	0.0
Uruguay	29.9	-55.5	22.1	37.2	0.0
Luxembourg	43.3	-63.2	-22.0	15.7	0.0
Paraguay	23.7	-88.6	-46.6	3.0	0.0
Lesotho	5.7	-95.7	-79.9	0.1	0.0
Singapore	314.8	-92.7	-73.2	0.0	0.0

Note: Negative entries indicate that hypothetical produced assets would be lower than observed assets under the specified rule.

7. Deforestation: accounting for a multiple-use resource

INTRODUCTION

The primary goal of this chapter is to extend the savings analysis to a domain that seems both particularly topical and important, the depletion of forests in the developing world. Green national accounting can inform this debate in a number of ways. Firstly, there is the provision of a consistent and coherent framework for analysing detailed and diverse data describing the net welfare cost of clearing forested land. Secondly, given the focus of these accounts on the better measurement of income and wealth, they are ideally suited to evaluating whether the switch of land use from forest to agriculture is actually wealth increasing (or 'sustainable'). Central to this is an expansion of the asset boundary to account explicitly for changes in land use, that is, where land is an asset that has a distinct (social) value depending on the use to which it is put (Hartwick, 1992, 1993; Vincent, 1999a).

A number of empirical studies have examined forestry and the national accounts (see, Vincent and Hartwick, 1997, for a comprehensive survey). Many of these studies, however, have focused exclusively on accounting for the net accumulation of timber that arises when forested land is cleared. The basic model underlying these calculations views the exploitation of primary forest as akin to a 'timber mine' where 'reserves' can be augmented via natural growth (Nordhaus and Kokkelenberg, 1999). Net accumulation is defined as net harvest (or net growth) valued at the unit rent or stumpage value for a given timber resource (see, for example, Repetto et al., 1989; van Tongeren et al., 1993; Seroa da Motta and Ferraz, 2000). A relatively sophisticated treatment of this problem is Vincent (1999b) which takes account of the age class of timber on a unit of land as well as the volume of resource harvested.

Where forested land provides benefits in addition to timber, understanding the loss of asset value on cleared land extends beyond the net accumulation of timber. Indeed, in acknowledgement of this, a number of studies have constructed accounts that encompass this wider notion of land value across a range of developed and developing countries. Thus, forestry accounts exist for non-timber forest products (NTFP) (Bartelmus et al., 1993; Hultkrantz, 1992; Hoffrén, 1996; Scarpa et al., 2000), environmental services such as watershed services and soil conservation functions (Aguirre, 1996; van Tongeren et al., 1993; Hamilton, 1997; Hassan, 2000; Torres, 2000) and fuelwood (Peskin, 1989; Katila, 1995). Fewer studies have estimated the value of biodiversity, although Hultkrantz (1992) proposes an estimate for Sweden based on the opportunity costs of conserving land. More recently, Haripriya (2000) accounted for the pharmaceutical benefits of forests in India based on an estimate of option value. A particularly novel treatment is Vincent et al. (1993) for Malaysia, which seeks to value species extinction. Several studies such as, for example, Hassan (2000) attempt to account for the value of net carbon accumulation or sequestration, with Anielski (1992) providing one of the first accounts of this type for Canada.

The remainder of this chapter is organized as follows. Firstly, in response to the primary conclusion of Vincent and Hartwick (1997: 50) that, 'empirical efforts to incorporate forest resources into the national accounts must be guided by economic theory more than they have been', we begin with an extended national accounting model of deforestation arising from slash-and-burn farming. Secondly, we provide an empirical application of some of the most important of the diverse changes in asset values described by this model. This case study illustrates the clearing of tropical rain forest in Peru and the competing market and non-market (net) changes in land assets that occur when forests are cleared. Thus, the contribution of the current chapter is to combine forests, non-market valuation and the theory of extended national accounting.

ACCOUNTING FOR EXCESS DEFORESTATION

While the bulk of this chapter is concerned with empirical estimation of an 'adjusted' national saving, it is important to place the empirical work in the relevant theoretical context. We therefore extend the models of Hartwick (1992) for income measurement with deforestation to include such issues as carbon dioxide (CO_2) sequestration, local and global preferences for standing forests, and production externalities associated with standing forests.

In common with Weitzman (1976), Hartwick (1990) and Mäler (1991), national income here is defined along the optimal path of a growth model for a simple economy with tropical forest. For the study nation we assume that there is a fixed amount of land that can either be used for agriculture (A, measured in hectares) or is covered by forest (L), and that deforestation is the process of conversion of some amount of forest land into agricultural land. The area deforested each year d is initially covered with a forest stock of density S/L (in cubic metres per hectare), where S is the total stock of timber. On forested land the amount of harvest is given by R.

Standing forest grows according to a function $g(S,L,X)$, with g_S following the usual pattern of being positive, then zero, then negative (that is, for a fixed L the growth curve is an inverted 'U' which defines a maximum sustainable yield and a long-run equilibrium growth rate of zero), while $g_L > 0$. X is the global stock of carbon dioxide (CO_2). This CO_2 fertilizes forest growth, so that $g_X > 0$. CO_2 dissipates naturally as described by the function $n(\eta X)$, where η is the share of the study country in the total global stock of CO_2.

Slash-and-burn is the assumed forest clearance mechanism in the study country. It is assumed that each cubic metre of timber yields α tonnes of CO_2 when burned, and symmetrically, that the growth of one cubic metre of timber absorbs α tonnes of CO_2 (in other words, the only source of carbon in trees is assumed to be atmospheric). The accounting identity for the stock of CO_2, given deforestation, natural growth and dissipation is therefore,

$$\dot{X} = \alpha \frac{S}{L} d - \alpha g - n(\eta X). \tag{7.1}$$

This represents the net addition to global carbon stocks as a result of current *and past* slash and burn (recall that ηX is the country's share of the total global carbon stock). Deforestation is assumed to cost an amount $f(d)$ of an aggregate good that can be consumed, invested or spent on deforestation. The production accounting identity is therefore given by,

$$F(K, A, R, L) = C + \dot{K} + f(d). \tag{7.2}$$

Total production depends on produced capital, agricultural land, timber harvest and the area of forested land (the latter can be conceived as a production externality, such as the water regulation services provided by upland forests). It is assumed that residents of the nation value consumption and standing forest, and that the rest of the world derives benefits from the existence of the forested area in the study nation. The stock of CO_2 causes harm both locally and globally. Therefore, the utility function for the forestry model is $U = U^1(C,L,X) + U^w(L,X)$, with $U_X < 0$ and where U^I and U^W refer to the utility of residents of the study nation and the rest of the world respectively.

For a fixed pure rate of time preference r for both residents and the rest of the world, the optimal growth model for this economy is specified as,

$$\max_{C,R,d} W = \int_0^\infty U e^{-rt} dt \quad \text{subject to:}$$

$$\dot{K} = F - C - f$$

$$\dot{A} = d$$

$$\dot{L} = -d$$

$$\dot{S} = -R - \frac{S}{L} d + g$$

$$\dot{X} = \alpha \frac{S}{L} d - \alpha g - n$$

For shadow prices γ_i for the stocks K, A, L, S and X, the current value Hamiltonian for this problem is,

$$H = U + \gamma_1 \left(F - C - f \right) + \left(\gamma_2 - \gamma_3 \right) d + \gamma_4 \left(-R - \frac{S}{L} d + g \right)$$

$$+ \gamma_5 \left(\alpha \frac{S}{L} d - \alpha g - n \right). \tag{7.3}$$

The first order conditions for this growth problem are:

$$\frac{\partial H}{\partial C} = 0 = U_C - \gamma_1 \quad \Rightarrow \gamma_1 = U_C \tag{7.4}$$

$$\frac{\partial H}{\partial R} = 0 = \gamma_1 F_R - \gamma_4 \quad \Rightarrow \gamma_4 = U_C F_R \tag{7.5}$$

$$\frac{\partial H}{\partial d} = 0 = (\gamma_2 - \gamma_3) - \gamma_1 f' - \gamma_4 \frac{S}{L} - \gamma_5 \alpha \frac{S}{L}$$

$$\Rightarrow (\gamma_2 - \gamma_3) = U_C f' + U_C F_R \frac{S}{L} + \gamma_5 \alpha \frac{S}{L}. \tag{7.6}$$

From the first-order conditions we can re-write the current value Hamiltonian in expression (7.3) as,

$$H = U + U_C \dot{K} + \left(U_C f' + \left(\alpha \gamma_5 + U_C F_R \right) \frac{S}{L} \right) d - U_C F_R \left(R + \frac{S}{L} d - g \right)$$

$$+ \gamma_5 \left(\alpha \frac{S}{L} d - \alpha g - n \right).$$

Collecting terms, the Hamiltonian may be written as current welfare plus the value of changes in the various assets: $U + U_C G$, where G is net or 'genuine' saving. If we define the marginal damages[1] from carbon dioxide to be $b \equiv - \gamma_S / U_C$, the expression for genuine saving is:

$$G = \dot{K} + \left(f' + \left(\alpha b + F_R \right) \frac{S}{L} \right) d - F_R \left(R + \frac{S}{L} d - g \right) - b \left(\alpha \frac{S}{L} d - \alpha g - n \right).$$

$$(7.7)$$

The last term in expression (7.7) is the value of damages from the net accumulation of CO_2 in the atmosphere. Slash-and-burn therefore adds to the CO_2 stock, while the growth of timber on the remaining forested land and natural dissipation of atmospheric CO_2 reduces it. The preceding term is the value of net reduction in the stock of timber. This has two components: net harvest of timber on forested land $(R - g)$; and timber burned on deforested land $(S/L \times d)$. Preceding that is the term representing the difference in the shadow prices of agricultural land and forested land. Here, marginal clearance costs (f'), damages from carbon dioxide emissions (αb) and the rental value of the timber that was burned are all part of the difference in prices between these two different uses of land.

It is also worth noting how global preferences for standing forest relate to the expression for genuine saving G in expression (7.7). Land is an asset which can be used for crop production or standing forest. In turn, the price of land under these distinct uses will depend on different factors. In particular, we can infer more about what factors determine these prices if we examine the steady-state conditions in expressions (7.8) and (7.9) below. If land at the frontier is assumed to be progressively less productive under agriculture (that is, $F_{AA} < 0$), while the marginal value under forests is not declining, then it is reasonable to assume that there will be a long run steady state with zero deforestation. In expression (7.8), we can see that γ_2, the (steady-state) shadow price of agricultural land, is related to the marginal returns to agricultural land (F_A). In expression (7.9), γ_3, the (steady-state) shadow price of forestland, is related to a range of factors such as the welfare enjoyed by citizens in the rest of the world from a hectare of land under standing forest (U_L^W).

At the margin in the steady state, if land clearance is costless, we would expect the value of land under these two competing uses to be equal. In other words, for the marginal hectare, we would expect that (in the steady state) $\gamma_2 = \gamma_3$ and that farmers are indifferent between land clearance and forest conservation (that is, the marginal benefits of clearance are just equal to the marginal costs). When land clearance is costly there is some additional term reflecting investment in land-use change that must be taken account of. In terms of our forestry model, it can be recalled from expression (7.7) that this investment term is related not only to marginal clearance costs (f') but to damages from carbon dioxide emissions (αb) and the rental value of the timber that was burned. This term drives a wedge between the value of land used for agricultural production and value of land under standing forest. Hence, if land clearance is costly, and we observe deforestation (that is, $d > 0$) then we can reasonably assume that agricultural returns, less the costs of that investment, must at least just equal the returns from keeping the land under standing forest.

Expression (7.7) is the expression for saving that we would expect to prevail if deforestation were optimal. However, there are good reasons to argue that the saving measure that we should be interested in is one where deforestation is non-optimal. Thus, in the real world we would expect that a variety of policy distortions and market imperfections can easily lead to *excess* deforestation. In the current context, 'excess' can be interpreted as deforestation yielding a decline in the social value of the land.

To characterize 'excess deforestation', it helps to explore the long run steady state where the agricultural frontier has stopped expanding.[2] At this point the marginal returns to agriculture must just equal the marginal returns to standing forest. This can most straightforwardly be done by examining the following dynamic first order conditions. First recall that the expression for $\gamma_2 - \gamma_3$ can be written as follows, after substituting in the expression for b:

$$(\gamma_2 - \gamma_3) = U_C(f' + (F_R + b\alpha)\frac{S}{L}).$$

The dynamic first order conditions for these shadow prices are given by:

$$\dot{\gamma}_2 = r\gamma_2 - \frac{\partial H}{\partial A} = r\gamma_2 - U_C F_A \tag{7.8}$$

$$\dot{\gamma}_3 = r\gamma_3 - \frac{\partial H}{\partial L} = r\gamma_3 - U_L^W - U_L^I - U_C F_L - U_C F_R g_L - U_C b\alpha g_L. \tag{7.9}$$

These are the standard first order conditions for the maximization problem. In what follows, we are interested in how these conditions can be used to define 'excess deforestation' and therefore genuine saving away from the optimum. Subtracting expression (7.8) from expression (7.9) and substituting the expression for $\gamma_2 - \gamma_3$ gives,

$$\dot{\gamma}_2 - \dot{\gamma}_3 = rU_C(f' + (F_R + b\alpha)\frac{S}{L})$$
$$+ U_C(F_L + F_R g_L + b\alpha g_L - F_A) + U_L^W + U_L^I. \qquad (7.10)$$

We define one more dynamic first order condition for the shadow price of produced capital, $\gamma_1 = U_C$:

$$\dot{\gamma}_1 = r\gamma_1 - \frac{\partial H}{\partial K} \quad \Rightarrow \quad \frac{\dot{U}_C}{U_C} = r - F_K \qquad (7.11)$$

This is just the Ramsey rule, and it implies that $r = F_K$, the interest rate, in the steady state. Therefore expression (7.10) reduces to the following in the steady state:

$$F_K(f' + (F_R + b\alpha)\frac{S}{L}) + F_L + F_R g_L + b\alpha g_L + \frac{U_L^W}{U_C} + \frac{U_L^I}{U_C} - F_A = 0 \qquad (7.12)$$

which can be rewritten as follows,

$$\frac{U_L^W}{U_C} + \frac{U_L^I}{U_C} + F_L + F_R g_L + \alpha b g_L + F_K \left(f' + (\alpha b + F_R)\frac{S}{L} \right) = F_A. \qquad (7.13)$$

The terms in expression (7.13) are relatively simple to interpret. Starting with the left-hand side of the expression, the first two terms are, respectively, the (marginal) willingness to pay (WTP) of foreigners[3] and national residents for a unit of standing forest. F_L is the production externality provided by a unit of forest. $F_R g_L$ is the rental value of the natural growth of forest on a unit of land – this is the sustainable harvest or off-take. $\alpha b g_L$ is the value of the carbon sequestered during natural growth on a unit of land. The next term is interest that would be earned if the sum of the clearance cost, carbon sequestration benefits and timber rental value for the marginal unit of deforested land were put in a bank. The sum of these terms on the left-hand side is the social value of a marginal hectare of forested land. Finally, the right-hand side is the marginal product of the unit of land under agriculture: that is, agricultural returns per hectare.

If for a given hectare of land the left-hand side of expression (7.13) is greater than the right, then there is excess deforestation. If it is assumed that there are d^* such hectares, that the land-use change is permanent, and that the interest rate F_K is constant, then the asset value of excess deforestation is given as,

$$\left(\frac{U_L^I}{U_C} + \frac{U_L^w}{U_C} + F_L + F_R g_L + \alpha b g_L + F_K\left(f' + (\alpha b + F_R)\frac{S}{L}\right) - F_A\right) \cdot \frac{d^*}{F_K}. \quad (7.14)$$

Expression (7.14) is the value of dissaving under excess deforestation, and therefore should be subtracted from expression (7.7) to arrive at genuine saving G. If it is assumed that all deforestation is excessive, so that $d = d^*$, then this subtraction yields,

$$G = \dot{K} - F_R\left(R + \frac{S}{L}d^* - g\right) - b\left(\alpha\frac{S}{L}d^* - \alpha g - n\right)$$

$$- \left(p_L^I + p_L^W + F_L + F_R g_L + \alpha b g_L - F_A\right) \cdot \frac{d^*}{F_K} \quad (7.15)$$

where, $p_L^I = U_L^I/U_C$ and $p_L^W = U_L^W/U_C$.

This analysis is a long route to a result that environmental economics would lead one to expect: that there is excess deforestation if the total value of forested land exceeds the return of the same land under agriculture. It is important, however, to consider the welfare implications of this measure of saving.

We know from Chapter 2 that on the optimal path $U_C G = \dot{W}$, where G is genuine saving and W is the present value of utility. The genuine saving measure inherent in expression (7.7) is therefore an indicator of whether the present value of utility is rising or falling along the optimal path. Moreover, negative genuine saving implies that the level of utility over some interval of time in the future must be less than current utility – development is not sustained, to use Pezzey's (1997) terminology.

Because the genuine saving measure inherent in expression (7.15) is not on the optimal path, there is no simple welfare interpretation. As long as the distortions in the economy do not have large impacts on calculated shadow prices,[4] we can say that, *ceteris paribus*, decreasing excess deforestation will increase genuine saving. The saving measure is therefore a useful performance indicator for policies that aim to approach the social optimum.

EMPIRICAL APPLICATION

Our study country is Peru where the rate of deforestation over the period 1990–95 was approximately 0.3 per cent per annum, compared to an average for Latin America of some 0.5 per cent over the same period (World Resources Institute, WRI, 1998). In terms of the extent of forest cleared, Peru's deforestation rate is estimated to be approximately 210 000 hectares per year (ibid.). For the purposes of applying our accounting framework, we draw on data from a number of sources and wherever possible we restrict attention to relevant Peruvian data (rather than 'similar' data transferred from elsewhere).

The total value of excess deforestation is a present value such that the value of the net change in forested land asset is the discounted sum of all future net losses attributable to switching land use on a unit of land. For example, when a hectare of forest is cleared these net conservation benefits – that is, components of the last term on the right-hand side of expression (7.15) are lost in perpetuity. Hence, annual estimates of losses must be converted to present values using some discount rate.

In principle, in our model, F_K is equivalent to the mean future value of the social rate of time preference $(SRTP)$.[5] In a fixed-technology neoclassical world, this social discount rate would decline to the pure rate of time preference in the long-run steady state. However, as a practical matter, setting F_K equal to the current social discount rate might be a working assumption. The $SRTP$ is the sum of the rate of impatience and the rate of decline in the marginal utility of consumption associated with an extra unit of consumption (for example, Lind and Schuller, 1998). This can be expressed in the following formula:

$$SRTP = r + \theta.\left(\dot{C}/C\right).$$

Here r is the pure rate of time preference (or rate of impatience, the rate at which future utility is discounted), θ is the elasticity of the marginal utility of consumption, and $\dot{C}/C$ is the percentage rate of growth in per capita consumption.

In practice, the appropriate value that this social discount rate should take is not obvious. That is, a project to clear a unit of forest land leads to both domestic (or local) and global net changes, which typically might be discounted at different rates. Assuming that the value should be based on a social discount rate for Peru and approximating $\dot{C}/C$ as the growth rate of (real) GNP per capita in Peru, annual growth over the period 1961 to 1999 was, on average, 1 per cent (World Bank, 2002a). However, this growth rate conceals much variation since the average annual growth rate of per capita GNP exceeded 2.5 per cent over the period from 1961 to the mid-1970s, was negative over the late 1970s and the 1980s and then approached 2.5 per cent again over the 1990s. Taking this 2.5 per cent growth rate as being indicative of future prospects in Peru and assuming that r lies between 0 and 2 and θ lies between 1 and 2 (Lind and Schuller, 1998; Pearce and Ulph, 1999) then this suggests a Peruvian social discount rate in the range of 1.25 per cent to 6 per cent. In what follows, we base our estimates, where necessary, on a social discount rate of 5 per cent. Our foregoing model assumes that, for example, the benefits of forest conservation are lost in perpetuity. Clearly, this creates a number of empirical issues not least by making any calculations relatively sensitive to the choice of discount rate. Rather than assume that such values are lost in perpetuity, in practice we will assume that the lifetime for calculating present values is 20 years. While it is worth noting that this assumption results in a conservative estimate of the net costs of deforestation, we comment in more detail below about the sensitivity of discounted parameters to changes in assumptions about the magnitude of the discount rate and the choice of a 'cap' for calculating present values.

In what follows, firstly we estimate those components of expression (7.15) – in per hectare terms – relating to timber burned on converted land and net accumulation of carbon. Secondly, we estimate those components of expression (7.15) – again, in per hectare terms – which we have identified as making up 'excess deforestation'.

Timber Depletion

The value of current timber rents is equivalent to the net growth of timber $(R - g)$ valued at its rental rate (F_R). This rental rate or stumpage value can be most simply estimated by the net price technique: that is, the (the border) price of timber minus the marginal costs of harvest and processing (including a normal return to capital, ROC). In practice, marginal production costs are almost never available and practitioners typically fall back on using average harvesting costs, which typically will tend to overstate calculated rents. This caveat aside, Table 7.1 illustrates the data we use to calculate current timber rents with regards to the timber price for Peru and the costs of harvest and processing activities in the Peruvian Amazon (in the Pucallpa and Von Humboldt areas).

World Bank (2002a) calculates the implicit export price of timber for Peru (from data on the value and volume of roundwood exports). In 1995, this (implicit average) current export price was $52.86/m^3$ in Peru. Average harvest costs are approximately 37 per cent of price (including a normal rate of return on capital) with transportation and loading accounting for most of these costs along with haulage. Deducting these unit costs from price of a cubic metre of timber gives a unit rental rent of $33.12. Regarding the volume of harvestable timber, a representative hectare in the

Wealth, welfare and sustainability

Table 7.1   Unit timber resource rents, 1995

	Dollar per cubic metre ($/m^3)
Unit (export) price	52.86
Costs	19.74
Locating/marking trees	0.13
Felling/blunting	0.78
Haulage	5.68
Log making	0.17
Loading	0.63
Transport	9.71
+ 5% ROC	2.64
Unit rent	33.12

Sources: Nalvarte (1999); World Bank (2002a).

von Humboldt region of the Peruvian Amazon contains about 113.5m^3 of timber biomass (FIL, 1975). However, it is unlikely that all of this unit volume is commercially valuable. Thus, timber harvested on forested land in Peru typically consists of timber of relatively high commercial value (for example, caoba (mahogany), cedro (cedar), ishpingo and tornillo) and various hardwoods and softwoods of relatively medium or low value (for example, cumala, sapote and huayruro). Evidence suggests that approximately 56.3m^3 of available timber is commercially valuable (FIL, 1975; Rivera, 1985) of which about 80 per cent (that is, 45m^3) is available subsequent to activities such as trimming (OAS et al., 1987). Multiplied by the rental rate per cubic metre of roundwood, the value of timber depletion on a unit of land is $1 491.72/ha.

Net Carbon Accumulation

The accumulation of a unit of CO_2 in the (global) atmosphere is akin to an addition to a (global) liability. Specifically, this change is equivalent to the present value of the future damage arising from net CO_2 accumulation when a hectare of forest is cleared.[6] Boscolo et al. (1997) propose a methodology that can be adapted here in order to estimate the net CO_2 (or equivalent carbon) emitted when slash-and-burn farmers clear forested land. In this approach, net carbon accumulation (NCA) is the difference in the (discounted) CO_2 stock over time for slash-and-burn (land use, j) and forest conservation (land use, i).[7] Mourato and Smith (2002) have reviewed available data on carbon accumulation for Peru (and surrounding countries) and we draw on these data in what follows. This evidence suggests that, on average, forest stores some 180tC/ha in above ground biomass with a further 36tC/ha in root biomass below ground. Crops and fallows are estimated to accumulate biomass at the annual rate of 12tC/ha above and below ground.

In our model, there are two additional elements of net carbon accumulation. The first, $b \times \alpha \times g$, is the value of carbon sequestered on remaining forestland in Peru. The second, $b \times n$, is the dissipation of Peru's 'share' of the global carbon stock. We do not consider the calculation of either of these magnitudes further in this chapter. For the latter, it is reasonable to assume that Peru's share of historical global CO_2 emissions can be thought of as being trivially small and that dissipation of the global atmospheric CO_2 is relatively slow (Hamilton and Clemens, 1999). However, the former may well be a non-trivial amount (see, for example, Haripriya, 2003) and thus this caveat should be noted.

Recent reviews by Tol et al. (2001), Pearce (2003) and Tol (2003) have sought to take stock of the available evidence about the 'most likely' (or best guess) estimates of the social costs of carbon. As an illustration of these findings, the conclusions of Pearce (2003) are summarized in Table 7.2. In the base-case, the best guess lies in the range of $5/tC to $10/tC (in 1995 prices). This range is lower than indicated by 'first generation' estimates: a finding which is largely attributable to more sophisticated treatments of adaptation (particularly in the agricultural sector) in recent estimates. However, other notable developments in the literature have served to boost estimates of the social costs of carbon. Two of these developments in particular are worth considering in more detail.

Table 7.2   Estimates of marginal damage of carbon emissions in $/tC (1995 prices)

	Carbon damage ($/tC)	
	Low	High
Base case	5	10
Equity weighting	5	25
Base with time-varying discounting	7	18
Equity weighting with time-varying discounting	7	44

Source: Pearce (2003).

Firstly, beginning with Fankhauser et al. (1997), the incorporation of explicit judgements about equity has been a distinguishing feature of recent efforts to value climate change. From Table 7.2, weighting damage values according to a country's relative per capita income, gives rise in the aggregate to a likely range of \$5/tC to \$25/tC.[8] Secondly, it is well known that the magnitude of the (social) discount rate has a significant bearing on estimates of the social cost of carbon (for example, Tol et al., 2001). More recently, a number of climate change studies have examined non-constant (that is, time-varying) social discounting (see, for a recent review, Groom et al., 2005). Time-declining discount rates – by slowing the rate of decline in discount factors – give greater weight to climate change impacts that occur in the distant future. Pearce (2003) argues that this has the effect of roughly doubling estimates of the social cost of carbon (relative to the base-case) and extends the range of values from \$7/tC to \$18/C. Hence, combining these two recent analytical concerns gives rise to damage estimates in the range of \$7/tC to \$44/tC (Table 7.2, final row). The range indicated in Table 7.2 accords with recent contributions by Tol et al. (2001) and Tol (2003) where it is argued that damage values in excess of \$50/tC are not justified in that these, for example, take overly strong ethical positions (for example, positions not easily reconciled with revealed social behaviour).[9]

Selecting an estimate even from the most likely ranges suggested by this literature is not straightforward; for example, in the current context, care should be taken to ensure consistency with assumptions (for example, about the path of discount factors) used elsewhere in the analysis. While there is considerable uncertainty about the likely magnitude of climate change, a number of recent assessments have concluded with 'likely' ranges towards the lower end of that indicated in Table 7.2. Perhaps most significantly, a large-scale meta-analysis of past climate change damage studies by Tol (2003) concludes with a best guess meta-estimate of \$10/tC to \$20/tC. Given that this study is the only detailed meta-analysis of findings to date we adopt both of these values in what follows.

Table 7.3   Value of net accumulation of carbon, 1995 (\$/tC/ha)

	Pasture		Secondary forest	
	$b = \$10$	$b = \$20$	$b = \$10$	$b = \$20$
$b\alpha(S/L)$	1938.83	3878.91	878.30	1805.88

Note: The value of b is assumed to rise at a constant rate of roughly 1% per annum following Fankhauser (1994).

Table 7.3 describes estimates of the dollar value of $b\alpha(S/L)$ or NCA per hectare of land. Our estimates of net carbon accumulation is, for $F_K = 5\%$,

b = \$10/tC or \$20/tC, and use of the land as pasture after slash-and-burn farming, in the range of \$1939/ha to \$3879/ha. The data in Table 7.3 also test the sensitivity of these estimates to changes in assumptions about whether land is converted to pasture or secondary forest after slash-and-burn farming on that land has ceased. Clearly, the final designation of land is crucial to our estimate of $ba(S/L)$. That is, for a given value of b, the magnitude of the debit attributable to net carbon accumulation for (final-use) pasture exceeds that for (final-use) secondary pasture by more than a factor of 2.

Excess Deforestation

Agricultural productivity

Converting land to agriculture under slash-and-burn farming is not the same as receiving a return in perpetuity and so our model is only indicative of this aspect of the land conversion process. The returns to a representative hectare of agricultural land must rather account for the mix of crops grown on that hectare by slash-and-burn farmers over the (finite) productive life of the soil. Hence, agricultural returns (π) under slash-and-burn farming are defined as follows:

$$\pi = F_{A_0} + \frac{F_{A_1}}{(1+F_K)} + ... + \frac{F_{A_T}}{(1+F_K)^T}.$$

That is, the present value of the return to agricultural production on a unit of land cleared in the current year comprises of the discounted (finite) stream of income that occurs from that year until the land is abandoned at T. In estimating this present value we use, as our starting point, data taken from the Pueblo Libre region of Peru – as broadly representative of agriculture in Peru – on physical yield per hectare per crop type on cleared land, the physical inputs used in crop production and the market prices of these outputs and inputs. These data all pertain to the year 1995 and are summarized in Table 7.4.

We assume that agricultural production, on a given hectare, takes place over approximately eight years as this appears to be typical of (slash-and-burn) farming practices in Pueblo Libre (Nalvarte, 1999). More specifically, in terms of the crops grown by slash-and-burn farmers in Peru, the first crop planted is typically rice, planted over two years. This is followed by a period of fallow (while another part of the farm is cleared and planted). After this period typically comes the planting of corn (maize) followed by plantain and yuca (cassava). Rice, corn and yuca all have a one-year growing cycle while plantain has a three-year growing cycle. Few, if any, capital inputs, aside from simple tools or fertilizer are used in slash-and-burn production. The most significant productive input is labour used in the cultivation of crops as well as initial clearing. This labour time is valued at the hourly agricultural wage with other inputs (capital, seed and so on) being valued at prevailing market prices.

Table 7.4   Basic agricultural data, 1995

	Output	Unit price (Nuevos Soles)	Labour (Days/ha/yr)	Wage (Nuevos Soles)	Capital	Unit cost
Rice	1333 kg	0.79	55	13.00	Seed 8 kg	1.00
					Seed service	100.00
Corn	1000 kg	0.35	25	13.00	Seed 12 kg	1.00
					Sack 20 units	0.30
Yuca	10000 kg	0.10	34	13.00		
Plantain	600 bunches	3.00	29	13.00		
Fuelwood	5000 kg		25	13.00		

Note: Exchange rate US$ = 2.25 Nuevos Soles.

Source: Nalvarte (1999).

Returns on a unit of agricultural land are highly likely to vary across hectares cleared for a number of reasons. An indication of these differences, by altitude and by geographical area (region), is provided in Table 7.5 (columns 1 to 4). These comparative data suggest that our estimates of yields in Pueblo Libre are relatively low for corn (compared to other areas), are marginally low for rice and yuca and slightly higher, on average, for plantain. Thus, it would be useful to take account of this variety in some way. One method of doing this could be to combine data on agricultural yields with data on the share of forest land or cleared land in each region. Columns 5 and 6 in Table 7.5 indicate that the locations described respectively account for about 78 per cent of forest land in Peru in 1995 and about 63 per cent of deforestation over the period 1990 to 1995.

Taking account of regional differences using these available data involves weighting crop yields in each region based on both its share of recent deforestation and remaining forest land.[10] Arguably this is a more satisfactory way of capturing regional differences than simply taking our field data on yields in Pueblo Libre as representative of the whole of Peru. However, it is itself imperfect in that, for example, it implicitly assumes that crop yields in remaining regions (that is, those not described in Table 7.5) correspond to the average. Nor was it possible to take account of the exact share of, say, highland and lowland forest in regions such as Ucayali (and so for practical purposes we have simply averaged the relevant data in column 1 in such cases).

Table 7.5   Agricultural crop production on cleared land by geographical location

	Rice (t/ha) (1)	Maize (t/ha) (2)	Yuca (t/ha) (3)	Plantain (t/ha) (4)	Per cent of forest land 1995 (5)	Per cent of cleared forest land 1990–95 (6)
Huánuco–Pueblo Libre: lowland	1.3	1.0	10.0	7.2	2.5	8.1
Huánuco–Puerto Inca: lowland	1.3	1.4	8.5	10.0		
Ucayali: lowland/ salt marsh	2.0	3.0	15.0	7.2	13.9	8.2
Ucayali: lowland	1.2	1.5	12.0	4.8		
Ucayali: highland	1.5	1.5	12.0	7.5		
Junín–Chanchamayo: highland	1.4	1.2	11.1	9.0	2.5	9.5
Junín–Satipo: highland	1.4	1.2	12.1	6.7		
Pasco–Oxapampa: highland	–	1.3	10.0	8.0	2.3	2.9
Loreto: lowland	2.3	1.5	10.4	10.4	51.4	15.0
San Martín: highland	5.1	2.1	12.8	8.0	5.2	19.5

Table 7.6 indicates the dollar value of a (regionally-adjusted) hectare of agricultural land, in terms of the (net) returns from the production of crops by slash-and-burn farmers. For a 5 per cent discount rate, agricultural returns are approximately $579/ha (compared to $370/ha if we were to base our data on Pueblo Libre alone).

Table 7.6   Agricultural returns on a representative unit of land

	Agricultural returns ($/ha) Central
Crop production	579.36
Fuelwood	242.30
Pasture	108.52
Present value (PV) of F_A	927.83

Notes:
Assumes 5% discount rate, 20-year lifetime for PV estimation.
Assumes pasture returns of $/ha per year of $17.5, $9 and $26 for central, low and high estimates respectively.

Source: Authors' own estimates from data in Nalvarte (1999).

It is important that the return to converting a hectare of land to agriculture should additionally take account of any productive value of the land when it is fallow and after the point at which the land is abandoned by the slash-and-burn farmer. In Table 7.6, the returns to fuelwood collection on fallow land are estimated assuming that each hectare of (fallow) land yields approximately 5 tonnes of fuelwood per year. This total harvest is valued at the opportunity cost of time spent collecting a unit of this resource: that is, hours spent collecting wood multiplied by the hourly agricultural wage. The table indicates that, for a 5 per cent discount rate, the present value of this harvest is $255/ha.

Regarding land use after the cycle of slash-and-burn crop production has finished, land may continue to earn a return if it is converted to pasture, for example, grazed by cattle (rather than left to revert to secondary forest). The extent to which deforested land is later converted to pasture varies across Peru. Clearly, however, it would be desirable to take some account of the value of pasture in our calculations. Unfortunately, there are no reliable data either from our study site or elsewhere in Peru that estimate the value of pasture. Schneidner (1995) reports estimates that the returns from pasture in the Brazilian Amazon are in the range of $8/ha to $24/ha per annum (in 1992). Hartwick (1993) estimates returns from pasture in Costa Rica (also for 1992) to be $9/ha per annum, towards the lower end of this range. We use data from Schneidner (1995) adjusted to 1995 prices which suggests a range of $9/ha to $26/ha with a central estimate of $17.5/ha. Table 7.6 illustrates that, for this mid-point value, the value of pasture is $109/ha. Taking the sum of agricultural production, fuelwood and pasture thus gives a present value of a unit of land of about $927.83/ha.

Local willingness to pay for conservation

Local people are assumed in our model to have preferences for standing forest, as well as consumption enjoyed by clearing these forests. Local willingness to pay to conserve a hectare of forested land is denoted by p_L^I. The underlying benefits upon which local people place value are diverse and might include air purification, maintenance of soil and water quality in addition to the provision of food (for example, game meat), shade and shelter (see, for example, van Kooten et al., 1999). Mourato and Smith (2002) value the local benefits to farmers in the Peruvian Amazon of moving from land use based on slash-and-burn agriculture to (increased) forest conservation. The study elicits farmers' (implicit) willingness to pay (WTP) for local conservation benefits using the contingent valuation method. Firstly, farmers were asked how much they would be willing to accept in compensation in order to conserve a unit of forested land rather than clear this land for slash-and-burn farming. Secondly, forest services were in effect 'sold back' as, in a follow-up question, farmers were asked how much they would be willing to reduce their stated compensation given that increased forest conservation provides them with environmental benefits.

Table 7.7   Local willingness to pay for conservation

	Central estimate	Lower bound	Upper bound
P_L^I	$67/ha	$55/ha	$72/ha
PV of P_L^I	$868.39	$712.86	$933.20

Note: Assumes 5% discount rate, 20-year lifetime for PV estimation.

Source: Adapted from Mourato and Smith (2002).

Mourato and Smith (2002) estimate that the implied mean local WTP per annum for conservation was $67/ha within a range of $55/ha to $72/ha. Table 7.7 illustrates that, for this central estimate, the present value of p_L^I is $868/ha (for $F_K = 5\%$). This lies in the range of $713/ha to $993/ha for the lower and upper bound estimates of p_L^I respectively. This would appear to be somewhat in excess of estimates of local benefits of tropical forests reviewed by, for example, Lampietti and Dixon (1995) and van Kooten et al. (1999). However, a recent review by Pearce et al. (1999) also makes it clear that this literature appears to offer a wide range of possible values, owing to differences in benefit coverage, study methodology and quality of existing studies.

Global willingness to pay for conservation

Global willingness to pay, p_L^W, has been characterized in the literature in a number of ways. One of the most commonly cited is non-use value where the global population might have preferences towards the existence of standing forest and its resident species, regardless of current or future use. Although there are a number of studies that directly value the non-use benefits of conserving specific species (or the implicit price of forest land based on donations to conservation groups), there are few examples that value the global benefits of forests. Indeed, the only example that we have found is Kramer and Mercer (1997) (henceforth, KM) who estimate the mean willingness to pay of US households to conserve 5 per cent of the world's remaining tropical rain forests.[11] KM's estimates of this non-use value yielded mean WTP of $26 per US household within the range of WTP of $8 and $40. It is important to note that this is a 'once-and-for-all' payment. Hence, respondents are assumed to discount the future benefits that they would receive from the conservation programme at some unknown (average) rate. We convert these data to 1995 prices using the dollar GDP deflator such that for present purposes the range we use is $9–$43 with a central estimate of $28 per household.

It would be useful to have a corresponding estimate for the WTP of households outside the US. In the absence of such data, the approach we take is to transfer US WTP, adjusted for per capita income (in PPP) differences, across (high-income) OECD[12] countries. For simplicity, we assume that the US ratio of population to households prevails across the OECD, which gives an estimate of approximately 300 million households. This generates an aggregate conservation 'fund' across the OECD of $2.2–$10.4 billion with a central estimate of about $6.7 billion. This is nearly 2.5 times a corresponding fund based on US households alone, indicating the importance of trying to include preferences for conservation of those resident in other (high-income) countries.

To estimate (the present value of) p_L^W, this 'fund' needs to be translated into an estimate of global WTP per unit (that is, per ha) of land. By dividing the product of WTP per household and total number of households by the number of hectares conserved under the proposed scenario, an estimate of this unit value is calculated. Assuming that KM's programme conserves an additional 46 million ha of forest[13] then global WTP is in the range of $47/ha to $225/ha with a central estimate of $147/ha.[14] This procedure is necessarily crude because not only does it rely on only one study of global preferences for forest conservation but also assumes that these preferences do not differ across high-income countries and that global WTP is constant across each unit of forest conserved. The latter is a particularly strong assumption. However, we invoke these assumptions in order to provide a placeholder for global conservation benefits within our framework.

Timber and carbon value of (forgone) sustainable harvest
For standing forest there is a sustainable off-take of timber that can be harvested while keeping the forest stock constant. The loss of this sustainable harvest in perpetuity is a component of excess deforestation: that is, the volume of natural growth of timber on forested land, g_L, valued at its unit rent, F_R. The physical volume of this yearly sustainable harvest can be equated to the mean annual increment (MAI) of the forest, the magnitude of which is dependent on biological (for example, tree species) and geographical (for example, climate, altitude) factors. Various estimates of natural growth or MAI have been presented in the forestry literature. For example, Solórzano et al. (1991) review a range of forest studies citing estimates in the range of 4.8 m³/ha and 20 m³/ha.

An important distinction is whether such estimates correspond to the growth rate of commercially valuable timber or, say, the total stock of woody biomass. Thus, a review by Nalvarte (1999) based on available literature and interviews with Peruvian forestry experts reports specific estimates of MAI for commercial timber which suggest considerably lower values, between 2m³ and 4.5m³. Hence, we use a conservative value of 2m³/ha as our estimate of the MAI for commercially valuable timber. Table 7.8 indicates that, on this basis, the value of this lost harvest is $858.5/ha. This is lower than the unit value of non-sustainable harvest, as would be expected (Pearce et al., 1999). In addition to its timber value, there is also a carbon value of the (forgone) sustainable harvest; that is, αg_L valued at carbon's shadow price b. On the assumption that 1m³ of timber contains (on average) 0.46/tC (Haripriya, 2003), the possible magnitude of the carbon value of the (lost) sustainable harvest for b = $10/tC, the present value of an annual 0.92/tC forgone is about $135.94/ha and is $267.10 if b = 20/tC.

GENUINE SAVING AND EXCESS DEFORESTATION

Table 7.8 summarizes our foregoing discussion of the value of excess deforestation. This assumes that slash-and-burn farming, our forestland clearance mechanism, is replaced by pasture, a discount rate of F_K = 5% and a 20-year period for the calculation of present values. This indicates that excess deforestation is $1082/ha or $1213/ha depending on whether the assumed value of b (the social cost of a tonne of carbon) is $10 or $20 respectively. Two points are worth noting in this respect. Firstly, the value of excess deforestation is smaller in magnitude than both the value of net timber accumulation, $F_R(S/L)$ and net carbon accumulation, $b\alpha(S/L)$. Secondly, regarding the components of excess deforestation it is evident that the sum of (present values of) $p_L^I + p_L^W$ (local and global WTP respectively), that is, \$1015/ha, is only a little in excess of agricultural returns, F_A. In other words, the estimated value of excess deforestation in the table is sensitive to the estimate of the timber and carbon value of the (forgone) sustainable harvest in that it is these values that 'tip' the balance such that the switch from forest to slash-and-burn agriculture can be characterized as, other things being equal, wealth-decreasing.

Table 7.8   Value of excess deforestation, 1995

	$b = \$10$	$b = \$20$
PV of:		
P_L^I	\$868.39	\$868.39
P_L^W	\$147.00	\$147.00
$F_R g_L$	\$858.50	\$858.50
bag_L	\$135.94	\$267.10
F_A	−\$927.83	−\$927.83
Value of excess deforestation	\$1082.00	\$1213.16

Note: Assumes 5% discount rate, 20-year lifetime for PV estimation.

Regarding the sensitivity of these findings to changes in key assumptions, the data are not notably sensitive to changes in assumptions about the magnitude of F_K; that is, unless assumed values are considerably lower or higher than 5 per cent. However, for our assumed value of F_K, placing a 20-year cap on calculating present values does have a significant effect on our findings; particularly on our estimates of p_L^I, $F_R(S/L)$, $b\alpha(S/L)$ relative to assuming that, when forest land is cleared, these values are lost in perpetuity. While, this latter assumption also has the effect of boosting our estimate of the gains to switching land use, by increasing F_A, a 20-year cap for calculating present values exerts an overall conservative influence on estimates of the net losses arising from deforestation.

In order to estimate genuine savings in Peru in 1995, the data in Table 7.8 are aggregated across total land deforested (d) and combined with other relevant national accounting data. The upper bound of d is the annual average deforestation rate over the period 1990 to 1995. Of course, this deforestation rate of 210 000 ha. refers to total deforestation not just land cleared for slash-and-burn farming and so the upper bound characteristic of this value should be noted in interpreting our results.[15]

Table 7.9   Genuine savings and deforestation in Peru, 1995

	Component of G, 1995 $d = 210\,000$	
	\$US million	% of GNP
S	\$11 354.8	19.9
$- dK$	\$6 977.9	12.2
$- \Sigma n_i Q_i$	\$850.3	1.5
$- F_R(S/L) \times d$	\$313.3	0.6
$- b\alpha(S/L) \times d$	\$407.2	1.4
$-$ Excess deforestation	\$254.8	0.5
of which PV of:		
P_L^I	\$182.4	0.3
P_L^W	\$30.9	0.1
F_{Rg_L}	\$180.3	0.3
bag_L	\$56.1	0.1
$-F_A$	\$194.9	0.3
= Genuine saving (G)	\$1 213.2	3.7

Notes: Assumes 5% discount rate, 20–year lifetime for PV estimation, b = \$20/tC.

Table 7.9 illustrates the components of genuine saving. Turning firstly to the forest-related changes in wealth, it can be seen that – for the upper bound case of d = 210 000 ha and where b = \$20/tC – the value of excess deforestation is \$255 million or equivalent to 0.5 per cent of GNP whereas the combined values of net timber accumulation and net carbon accumulation are about 2 per cent of GNP. The table also combined these forestry data with other non-forest variables relevant to the calculation of genuine saving, including gross savings (S), depreciation of produced capital (dK) and the depletion of non-renewable natural resources ($\Sigma n_i Q_i$): the product of the quantity extracted of resource i (Q_i) valued at its rental rate (n_i). These data can be found in World Bank (2002a). The magnitudes of these additional terms respectively as a percentage of GNP are 19.9 per cent, 12.2 per cent and 1.5 per cent.[16]

Genuine saving is defined in Table 7.9 as the rate of gross saving minus the depreciation of produced capital, non-renewable resource depletion and the depletion of forest resources (including the value of excess deforestation). Table 7.9 shows that, for d = 210 000, genuine savings is 3.7 per cent. Thus Peru appears to have avoided negative genuine savings in 1995 although the effect of subtracting various components of asset consumption significantly reduces the measured increase in total wealth for that year. In particular, the effect of accounting for the clearance of forest land is to reduce the genuine saving rate by an amount equivalent to 2.5 per cent. However, it is interesting to note that the value of excess deforestation appears to account for only about one-fifth of this amount. In particular, the (present) value of p_L^W lost on deforested land amounts to just 0.1 per cent of GNP.[17] In other words, other elements of forest land asset consumption are empirically more important. One implication of this finding is that although the value of excess deforestation is quantitatively significant, in terms of measuring the rate of genuine saving across the Peruvian economy the timber and carbon value of trees cleared are arguably more noteworthy determinants of (weak) sustainability.

The genuine saving calculation in Table 7.9 is an estimate of *total* saving effort. However, the Peruvian population is growing at a rate of 1.7 per cent per year. As shown in Hamilton (2002), performing the savings analysis in per capita terms requires two steps.[18] First, the calculation of genuine saving per capita, which is roughly $84 according to the findings previously discussed (for a population of 25.6 million). (It is worth noting, that forest-related items reduce genuine saving per capita by about $38.) Second, a 'wealth-dilution' term, representing the sharing of total wealth with this extra 1.7 per cent of the population in 1995, must be subtracted – this can be calculated to be about $131 in 1999 using the figures in Chapter 2. So we can conclude that genuine saving per person in Peru is arguably not robust, at $84, and that the change in wealth per capita is quite likely negative.

It is worth mentioning, however, that this approach neglects the notion of strong sustainability. This is characterized by Pearce et al. (1989) as the idea that there are some amounts of critical natural capital that must be preserved if welfare is to be maintained – there are essentially no substitutes for certain natural assets. Many experts and lay people alike would claim that tropical rain forests are critical stocks of living natural resources that provide life-support functions. One way of capturing this notion of a critical amount of rainforest, within our extended accounting framework is by assuming that,

$$U_L^W \to \infty \text{ as } L \to \bar{L}^+,$$

where $\bar{L}^+$ is the critical area – that is, as forested area declines to the critical amount, arbitrarily large losses in (global) welfare are associated with deforestation of a marginal hectare. The resulting excess deforestation would show up in our model as a large loss in land value. Thus, if global preferences are taken into account, the optimal programme will also be strongly sustainable, because the rapid increase in global willingness to pay will quickly reduce the amount of deforestation. While this approach can handle strong sustainability in principle, in practice it requires good measures of global willingness to pay for conservation and sufficient scientific and economic information (concerning the damages resulting from loss of rainforest) for preferences to reflect the appropriate trade-offs that would underpin this willingness to pay.[19]

CONCLUDING REMARKS

We have investigated how a developing country might green its national accounts for current 'excess' deforestation arising from slash-and-burn farming in theory and have illustrated how our framework can be implemented in practice. Our extended national accounting model has focused on a broad range of costs and benefits of deforestation. In particular, we have derived an accounting term reflecting excess deforestation – defined as the sum of the (present) values of sustainable timber harvest, local and global willingness to pay for conservation minus agricultural returns on deforested land. Using a range of market and non-market data, reflecting these changes, we have constructed an estimate of the genuine savings rate for Peru. This is based on the extended net saving rate derived from our model (that is, *NNP minus consumption*). Sustainability requires that genuine savings should not be negative in the aggregate.

Our calculations show that the Peruvian genuine savings rate in 1995 was 3.7 per cent of GNP (although the change in per capita wealth was in all likelihood negative because of population growth). The effect of accounting for (net) changes in wealth that arise when forest land is cleared for slash-and-burn farming is to reduce the estimated genuine savings rates by 2.5 percentage points. Yet, the value of excess deforestation itself only accounts for about one-fifth of this decrease. A number of points should be made in qualifying these findings. While our accounting model allows for the change in asset value on land cleared of forest to be specified in theoretically precise terms, in practice there is considerable uncertainty regarding the data needed to calculate these terms and, for example, the appropriate magnitude of discount rates. This gives rise to potentially wide ranges of values for much of the data, as we have discussed. As regards outstanding conceptual issues, there remains a need to investigate, in more detail, how the notion of strong sustainability can be accommodated into our analysis in both theory and practice.

Finally, with respect to policy implications, in our deforestation model local consumption (that is, forest clearance) decisions reduce welfare in other countries. In other words, the optimal mix of forest and agricultural land is different to that which currently prevails given that farmers, for some reason, cannot capture the value of conservation benefits. In reality, attempts to reduce excess deforestation will have to translate these values into transfers that farmers in Peru can appropriate. Such mechanisms, in essence, have been put into effect by the Global Environment Facility (GEF) and endorsed in international environmental agreements such as the Convention for Biodiversity. In this deforestation case, the property right (to the forest) lies with the forested country (and moreover, farmers). Thus, at least part of the reduction in genuine savings associated with excessive deforestation (from a global perspective) is linked to the extent to which compensation would be owed to the forested country if it reduced its deforestation to globally optimal levels. Our deforestation accounting problem therefore reinforces the rationale for actual mechanisms that transfer income to a forested country in order to reduce deforestation. However, it is useful to have the implications for green national accounting and sustainability made clear as well.

NOTES

1. Carbon dioxide is a global pollutant, but if a given property right regime is assumed – the right not to be polluted by your 'neighbour' – then valuing the global damage from CO_2 emissions in net saving is the correct accounting approach.
2. We are assuming, therefore, that deforestation is initially socially profitable, but that there are declining marginal returns to clearing for agricultural land, leading to the possibility of a steady state in the long run.
3. Note that this is only approximately foreign WTP, since we are dividing by the national marginal utility of consumption.
4. This seems reasonable when cleared timber is burned rather than sold on the market.
5. The *SRTP* is the fundamental discount rate in growth theory and can be defined as the maximum amount of extra consumption made possible by forgoing a unit of consumption now.
6. We assume, for simplicity, that the dissipation of Peru's 'share' of the global carbon stock is zero on the basis that Peru's share of historical global CO_2 emissions is trivially small and that dissipation of the global atmospheric CO_2 is relatively slow (Hamilton and Clemens, 1999).
7. CO_2 is discounted under the rationale that a unit of carbon emitted (or sequestered) in the future is less costly (or less valuable) than a unit of carbon emitted (or sequestered) in the present.
8. Not surprisingly, there is debate about the precise weights to assign or, indeed, whether any explicit weighting is desirable. For example, Pearce (2003) counsels against using 'unjustifiably' high estimates of inequality aversion: that is, values which appear to have no basis in actual decision-making as revealed say in aid distribution to the world's poor.
9. Of course, some uncertainty surrounds the likely influence on estimates of risks of catastrophic climate-related outcomes which are lacking in almost all studies to date (see, for an exception, Link and Tol, 2004).
10. This is calculated as the average of the share of remaining forest land in 1995 (column 5) and forest land cleared between 1990–95 (column 6). For example, for Ucayali, yields are weighted by the value: $0.5 \times [(0.139/0.778)] + 0.5 \times [(0.082/0.632)]$.

11. This is based on expert consensus that to maintain the integrity of the global rain forest ecosystem would require protection of 10 per cent of remaining forest, half of which is already currently under some form of protection.
12. See World Bank (1999) for a definition of high-income Organisation for Economic Co-operation and Development countries.
13. According to World Resources Institute (1998) this constitutes 5 per cent of the world's tropical forest in the year in which KM carried out their study.
14. If the magnitude of WTP was based on US households alone this range would be $18–$85 per ha.
15. In practice, alternative forest clearance mechanisms will vary in terms of their productivity, in the case say of large-scale commercial farming, or the loss of forest-derived environmental services, in the case say of agro-forestry production.
16. According to World Bank data, non-renewable resource rents were relatively high during the 1970s and 1980s – for example, between 4 and 18 per cent (with a period average of 9 per cent) reflecting the depletion of oil, copper and nickel. However, during the 1990s resource rents declined.
17. While this might seem to be 'too low' it should be noted that, say, an arbitrary threshold value of national significance of 1 per cent of GNP (used as an informal rule of thumb in some studies) implies a per hectare loss of in excess of $1000; well above those ranges suggested to date in the literature.
18. Dasgupta (2001) and Chapter 3 have set out the theory underlying this practical interest in changes in wealth per capita as a sustainability indicator.
19. Recent contributions that seek to identify and categorize critical natural capital such as Ekins et al. (2003) are interesting but tentative signs of progress with regards to this important policy question.

8. Accounting for technological change

INTRODUCTION

To what extent will delivering sustainable development depend critically on the rate of technological change? For example, questions surrounding the importance of technological improvements in enhancing economic prospects and how these improvements come into being have been a lively source of debate in the economic growth literature (see, for a review, Barro and Sala-i-Martin, 1995; Jones, 1998). Much of this discussion is highly relevant to the problem of sustainability; that is, the conditions for its achievement and the measurement of progress towards sustainable development.

It is perhaps surprising then that few proposed indicators of sustainability currently integrate technological change in any meaningful way. For example, the theory underpinning much of this literature, as for example outlined in chapters 2 and 3, is in large part a cautionary tale about the (net) accumulation of (per capita) total wealth rather than improvements in productivity. By and large, models which have been used to underline the importance of this savings approach have assumed, for simplicity, fixed technology, largely in order to examine critical but previously neglected measurement issues surrounding the liquidation of resource and environmental assets. If, in reality, there is technological change, estimates of income and saving based on these simple models may not accurately inform prospects for sustainable development.

This last point has been made forcefully in Nordhaus (1995), Weitzman (1997) and Weitzman and Löfgren (1997).[1] For example, in Weitzman and Löfgren, a green national accounting framework is extended in order to investigate the impact on current national accounting aggregates of future economic growth attributable to increased productivity. The resulting annuity term or premium – reflecting the dollar value today of future technological change – provides a boost to current estimates of income and saving. Indeed, the authors calculate that the magnitude of this technology premium for the United States (USA) could be as much as 41 per cent of its Gross National Product (GNP). This finding suggests profound implications for measuring sustainability; that is, it appears to suggest that not only does technological change play a significant role in determining

118

prospects for sustainable development, it could play the decisive role. Put another way, in terms of measuring sustainable development, estimates of the future benefits of technological change are likely to trump offsetting adjustments such as, for example, the value of changes in resource stocks and environmental liabilities.

Nevertheless, as we show in this chapter, this conclusion about the usefulness (or otherwise) of green national accounting is necessarily not a generality and, furthermore, arises as a logical consequence of applying one particular theoretical perspective about how improvements in productivity come into being. Specifically, it views technological change as *exogenous* and *costless*. An alternative approach that has received a great deal of recent attention in the literature on economic growth, in contrast, views this process (whereby technological change comes into being) as both *endogenous* and *costly*. Interestingly, the two approaches result in divergent conclusions about the relative worth of green national accounting; that is, the likely boost, on average, to current estimates of income and saving as a result of calculating premia across countries to reflect technological change. This necessitates a practical judgement as to which of these characterizations of technological change is the more fitting in the real world.

The remainder of this chapter is set out as follows. The second section outlines a conceptual framework for accounting for exogenous technological change and illustrates these arguments with data for a range of countries. The third section then explores the conceptual and practical implications of accounting for endogenous technological change. The final section provides a discussion concerning the relative importance of technological change in measuring genuine saving and comments on whether such change is better characterized as an exogenous or as an endogenous process.

EXOGENOUS TECHNOLOGICAL CHANGE

The effects of exogenous technological change on a measure of Net National Product (NNP) and its implications for sustainability have been analysed in some detail recently by, for example, Weitzman and Löfgren (1997). In what follows, the main results of the extended Hicksian approach for this problem are outlined and discussed (where in common with Weitzman (1976), Hartwick (1990) and Mäler (1991), national income is defined along the optimal path of a growth model for a simple economy). The full details of this approach and derivation of the NNP measure are provided in Appendix 8.1. It should be noted that it is this framework and its use that also underlies the results presented in this chapter.

For an economy with fixed population and labour force (which is therefore factored out of the model below), exogenous technological change is modelled by assuming that total factor productivity grows at some fixed rate g, so that the national accounting identity for gross national product (GNP) is,

$$GNP \equiv F(K,R,t) = Ae^{gt}K^{\alpha}R^{\beta} = C + \dot{K} + \delta K, \text{ for } \alpha + \beta < 1.$$

Here A represents total factor productivity, K capital, R resources, C consumption, and α and β the elasticities of output with respect to capital and resources respectively. It is assumed that resource extraction is costless and that the percentage rate of depreciation of produced assets is constant at δ. The optimal growth model is therefore,

$$\max W = \int_t^{\infty} U(C(s))e^{-\rho(s-t)}ds \text{ such that:}$$
$$\dot{K} = F(K,R,t) - C - dK$$
$$\dot{S} = -R.$$

Deriving the conditions for the optimal path and applying the Hicksian definition of national income leads to the following expression for *NNP*,

$$NNP = GNP - F_R R - dK + T. \tag{8.1}$$

where *NNP* is defined as *GNP* minus the value of resource depletion (the quantity of the resource extracted, R, valued at its rental rate, F_R) and the depreciation of produced capital (dK) plus a technological premium, T, reflecting the value of technological change. The premium in expression (8.1) is given by,

$$T = g\int_t^{\infty} F(K,R,s)e^{-\int_t^s (F_K(\tau)-\delta)d\tau}ds$$

and can be interpreted, therefore, as the present value of growth attributable to future technological improvements.[2] Weitzman and Löfgren (1997) have argued that plausible estimates of the final term in expression (8.1) are likely to be large; that is, far greater than the dollar value of say the sum of $F_R R$ and δK in many cases, as illustrated by their finding that this term is roughly equal to 41 per cent of GNP for the US. Similarly, Weitzman

(1997) asserts that, in general, even relatively conservative assumptions about productivity growth will generally have considerable implications for the conclusions about sustainability that can be derived from green national accounting exercises.

An evaluation of this claim across a range of countries is relatively straightforward if there are relevant data on total factor productivity (TFP) growth, g, the social discount rate and gross product. Thus, the premium T could then be simply calculated as the product of TFP growth, g, and national income divided by the social discount rate. This amounts to 'predicting' future income gains by projecting past evidence about technological change into the future:[3,4]

$$F_0 \cdot g/(\delta - g), \text{ where,}$$
F_0 is current GNP
δ is the social discount rate.

In empirical studies, the parameter g is typically defined as that portion of the rate of growth of output that cannot be accounted for by the growth rate of inputs (such as produced capital and labour) (see, for example, Barro and Sala-i-Martin, 1995). Thus, g is typically accounted for as a (growth) residual and so its magnitude depends not only on the ('true') rate of technological progress but also crucially on how capital and labour inputs are measured. For example, Jorgenson (1995) demonstrates that the estimated contribution of productivity growth to economic growth is significantly diminished when improvements in the quality (as well as the quantity) of heterogeneous capital and labour inputs are acknowledged as components of economic growth. Put another way, this has the effect of reducing the residual intended to capture the rate of technological change. Even so, this still accords some non-trivial, albeit smaller, role for technological change. For the US economy, Jorgenson (1995) finds that the TFP growth rate was 0.7 per cent over the period 1947 to 1985. Such a rate of growth would remain consistent with a potentially large technology premium.

Estimates of g in the results that follow are taken from Collins and Bosworth (1996) and are illustrated in Table 8.1 for a number of countries, geographical and economic groupings including China, South Asia and East Asia, the United States and other industrialized countries, Latin America and the Caribbean, Middle East and North Africa and Sub-Saharan Africa.[5] These data, derived from a growth accounting exercise, describe cross-country growth in TFP over the period 1960 to 1994 where productivity growth is defined as that proportion of economic growth which is not accounted for by changes in inputs *including* human capital. Data on

GDP and GNP (in 1997) as well as cross-country estimates of the social discount rate, which is pegged using an estimate of the social rate of time preference (SRTP) are taken from Hamilton (2000).

Table 8.1   Total factor productivity (TFP) growth rates, 1960–94

	TFP growth rate (g) (%)
China	2.6
East Asia	1.1
Indonesia	0.8
Korea, Rep.	0.8
Malaysia	0.9
Philippines	−0.4
Thailand	1.8
South Asia	0.8
USA	0.3
Industrialized countries (excl. USA)	0.8
Latin America and Caribbean	0.2
Middle East and North Africa	−0.3
Sub-Saharan Africa	−0.6

Source: Collins and Bosworth (1996).

Table 8.2 illustrates findings for the rough size of technology premia in China, South Asia and East Asia, the United States and other industrialized countries, Latin America and the Caribbean, Middle East and North Africa and Sub-Saharan Africa (see also Table 8A.1). Column 1 in the table shows that the magnitude of these estimates (expressed as a percentage of a grouping's GNP) lie in a wide range between 32.1 per cent (other industrialized countries) and −19.1 per cent (Sub-Saharan Africa). China's premium is 32.1 per cent despite having by far the largest estimated rate of growth in TFP. This is explained by the relatively high rate used to discount future growth attributable to technological change. For the USA, the estimated technological premium of 9.7 per cent is substantially lower than that in say Weitzman and Löfgren (1997). This is because the rate of TFP of 0.3 per cent estimated by Collins and Bosworth (1996) is considerably lower than the rate of 1.0 per cent used by those authors. If the latter value were adopted here this would result in a value of T of about 42 per cent (of US GNP); that is, almost identical to Weitzman and Löfgren's findings. In the

case of Middle East and North Africa and Sub-Saharan Africa, the findings
make clear the implications of reductions in TFP (that is, a negative rate
of growth). An estimated decrease in productivity means that any country
must actually augment its saving efforts (relative to the assumption of no
technological change) if, other things being equal, it is to sustain future
consumption or welfare.

*Table 8.2   Accounting for technological change: exogenous and
endogenous cases*

	Exogenous case		Endogenous case	Depletion/Depreciation	
	T_∞ as % of *GNP* (1)	T_{20} as % of *GNP* (2)	*D* as % of *GNP* (3)	$F_R R$ as % of *GNP* (4)	*dK* as % of *GNP* (5)
China	32.1	28.0	0.5	4.0	8.9
East Asia	17.4	13.2	1.3	2.1	10.6
Indonesia	8.8	8.0	0.1	6.5	5.2
Korea, Rep.	10.0	8.3	2.8	0.0	12.2
Malaysia	15.1	11.4	0.4	6.0	11.7
Philippines	−5.8	−4.5	0.2	1.4	8.2
Thailand	21.1	18.8	0.1	0.9	13.7
South Asia	16.1	10.6	0.7	4.0	9.2
USA	9.7	4.6	2.5	0.9	11.6
Industrialized countries (excl. USA)	32.2	12.8	2.2	0.3	14.1
Latin America and Caribbean	9.0	3.3	0.5	3.6	10.8
Middle East and North Africa	−8.5	−4.4	1.0	10.4	11.1
Sub-Saharan Africa	−19.1	−9.2	0.4	7.8	10.6

How do these estimates of *T* compare with the magnitude of resource
depletion ($F_R R$) and depreciation of produced capital (*dK*)? Column 4 in
Table 8.2 describes values for total resource rents expressed as a percentage
of GNP. These data are taken from World Bank (2003). Resources are
defined in World Bank (2003) to include energy resources (for example,
oil, gas and so on), mineral resources (copper, bauxite and so on) and
forest (timber) resources. Total resource rent or depletion, for each of these
resources, is defined as the product of a given resource's unit rent (that is,
its world price minus country-specific extraction costs) and total units or
quantity extracted (or harvested) in any year. Hence, it should be noted that
column 4 does not include changes in environmental liabilities (for example,
attributable to pollutants such as PM10). A comparison of the values in
columns 1 and 4 indicates that for those country groupings where *g*>0,

the value of a technology premium always exceeds the value of resource depletion. In other words, these data indicate that the impact on future well-being of liquidation of resource wealth is, on average, more than offset by productivity gains elsewhere in the economy. For the most resource abundant groupings (Middle East and North Africa and Sub-Saharan Africa), the technology premium is negative which, if taken at face value, indicates that depletion combined with decreased productivity of factors means that an even greater savings effort would be required if future well-being is to be sustained. Table 8.2 also provides a more detailed picture for the East Asia grouping. Thus for Indonesia and Malaysia where the value of resource depletion is equal to 6.5 per cent and 6.0 per cent (respectively) of GNP in 1997, the estimated value of the technology premium is significantly larger in the case of the latter country although marginally larger than depletion in the case of the former. However, viewed together with estimates of the depreciation of produced capital (column 5 in Table 8.2) a somewhat different story emerges in that, with the obvious exceptions of both other industrialized countries and China, T is either greater than the sum of $F_R R$ and dK or is broadly similar in magnitude.

The calculations underpinning the results in column 1 discussed above implicitly assume that the higher output arising from technological change is enjoyed 'forever' (while $SRTP>0$ ensures that this is a finite value). Hence, column 2 in Table 8.2 shows the sensitivity of capping the projected premium, T, at 20 years. For example, Pezzey et al. (forthcoming) employ this assumption on the basis that forecasts beyond this (for example, column 2) 'are very dubious'. The relevant expression here is:

$$\sum_{j=0}^{N-1} F_0 \cdot g \cdot \frac{(1+g)^j}{(1+\delta)^j}, \text{ where,}$$

N is the number of years over which the present value calculation is being made.

Whether there is a difference between results that emerge from different assumptions about the time period to project the benefits of productivity improvement will depend critically on the magnitude of the social discount rate. Hence, for China, East Asia and South Asia the divergence between estimates of technology premia in Table 8.2 (that is, columns 1 and 2) is arguably not startling. However, for the USA, other industrialized countries and Latin America and the Caribbean, the boost to genuine saving in column 2 is considerably lower, just as the debit for the Middle East and North Africa and Sub-Saharan Africa is lessened. Interestingly, for groupings where $g>0$, the value of the technology premium in column 2 (T_{20}) still exceeds the value of the resource depletion with the exception of Latin America and the Caribbean. However, apart from China and Thailand (within the East Asia grouping), the value of T_{20} is always less than the value of resource depletion and the depreciation of produced capital combined.

In summary, Table 8.2 indicates that, for a number of (but not all) countries, the likely approximate size of a premium to reflect the present value of future technological change could be a determining factor in assessments of sustainable development. Although not a generality, as we have seen, if technological change is truly costless ('like manna dropping from heaven') any adjustment of the savings rate to reflect resource depletion and so on is likely to be swamped by the effects of technological change for economies where the rate of growth of total factor productivity is strongly positive. However, it is interesting to ask to what extent this conclusion is based on the simplifying assumption that productivity growth is costless, as was assumed in the above analysis? That is, how might an alternative and plausible assumption that technological change is costly to bring about – that is, that some amount of a scarce resource must be used to create it – change recommendations about how to account for such change? It is to this question that we now turn.

ENDOGENOUS TECHNOLOGICAL CHANGE

Relaxing the assumption of exogenous and costless technological change does not imply that technological change is no longer important for sustaining development. However, from an accounting standpoint, this may raise novel measurement issues. Resources used in the creation of new knowledge are primarily conceived as inputs to the research and development (R&D) sector. The rate of technological change is now said to be *endogenous* and thereby affected by economic decisions such as the amount of skilled labour to be directed towards R&D or knowledge creating activities. An adaptation of a model by Takayama (1980) will be used to explore costly technological change in what follows. While the more recent literature on endogenous growth (see, for instance, Aghion and Howitt, 1998) has provided more sophisticated approaches to this problem, the simple Takayama model is sufficient to make the key point about national accounting.

We assume that there is a fixed amount of labour $\bar{L}$ that may be used either for production or in research and development (L_D), so the production function is

$$GNP = F = AK^{\alpha}R^{\beta}L^{\varepsilon} \text{ for } L = \bar{L} - L_D.$$

The percentage growth rate of total factor productivity ($\dot{A}/A$) is determined by an R&D effort function $\theta(L_D)$: that is, the product of the number of workers engaged in R&D (L_D) as well as their productivity in generating knowledge (θ).[6] Hence, the optimal growth model becomes,

$$\max W = \int_t^\infty U\big(C(s)\big)e^{-\rho(s-t)}dt \text{ such that:}$$
$$\dot{K} = F\big(K,R,L\big) - C - \delta K$$
$$\dot{S} = -R$$
$$\dot{A} = \theta\big(L_D\big)A.$$

An essential part of the programme is the choice of the optimal amount of R&D effort, so the rate of technological change is determined endogenously in this model. Deriving the first order conditions for the model and applying the Hicksian definition of income yields the following expression for *NNP*,

$$NNP = GNP - F_R R - \delta K + D. \tag{8.2}$$

The technological change premium, D, in expression (8.2) is given by,

$$D \equiv \frac{\theta}{\theta'} F_L.$$

If the research effort is linearly related to the share of R&D labour in the labour force then,

$$\theta\big(L_D\big) = \omega \frac{L_D}{L},$$

and for constant ω, the technological change premium is given by

$$D = \varepsilon \frac{L_D}{\bar{L} - L_D} F.$$

What is the likely empirical magnitude of this term, D, to reflect endogenous technological change? As a crude illustration, if the elasticity of output with respect to labour, ε, is roughly equal to 0.6 and the ratio of R&D labour to production labour is roughly 0.05 (a very high estimate), then a plausible value for the technological change premium is 3 per cent of GNP. This is substantially less than the 41 per cent of GNP that Weitzman and Löfgren (1997) estimate for the USA on the assumption of exogenous technological change.

Another way of thinking about the magnitude of D, in practice, is with reference to R&D expenditures. Expression (8.2) can then simply be interpreted as saying that research and development expenditure should be treated as investment in the national accounts. R&D expenditures would then be included in estimates as genuine saving. This is a similar finding to that of Pemberton and Ulph (2001) who demonstrate that if technological change is wholly endogenous and national accounts correctly measure the value of R&D inputs, no further adjustment need be made to either NNP or genuine saving. In other words, the endogenous component of technology is already captured by national accounts.[7] However, in practice, R&D expenditures are usually counted as intermediate or final consumption in national accounts. For example, the 1993 revision to the System of National Accounts (SNA93) (United Nations, 1993) does discuss the treatment of R&D expenditures with some care. However, while admitting R&D is like investment, SNA93 does not recommend treating it as investment in the accounts because of difficulties defining and measuring the corresponding asset created. The conventional treatment of R&D expenditures as consumption means that the value of D should be seen as a boost to existing estimates of genuine saving.

Table 8.2 (column 3) reports data on R&D expenditures (expressed as a percentage of GNP) for those same countries and groupings as in our previous discussion with regard to exogenous change. Data on R&D expenditures are taken from Hamilton (2002) and refer to the year 1997. Estimates of D in the table range from 2.5 per cent in the USA and 2.2 per cent in other industrialized countries to 0.5 per cent in Latin America and the Caribbean and 0.4 per cent in Sub-Saharan Africa. Thus, spending on R&D as a percentage of GNP is relatively low, on average, in low-income countries and relatively high, on average, in high-income countries. The magnitude of these estimates of R&D expenditures (relative to GNP) for all countries indicates that in contrast to the exogenous case, green national accounting remains an important tool to our understanding of sustainable development. That is, for those countries with resources, estimates of D are arguably not large relative to values of resource depletion.

DISCUSSION AND CONCLUSIONS

In this chapter, we have discussed the implications of accounting for technological change in the measurement of genuine or adjusted net saving.

Other things being equal, future generations will be better off, relative to the present, as a result of technological improvements. In this sense, technological change can largely be in part relied on to take care of the future subject to the caveat, added by Aghion and Howitt (1998), that policy fosters a general climate conducive to innovation effort and increases in productivity.

From an accounting perspective, if technological change is not bought and sold in markets then this benefit is not recorded in national accounts (Nordhaus, 1995). Hence, nor will it be reflected in measures of genuine saving based on national accounts. This observation does not mean that savings rules are no longer relevant to the measurement of sustainable development. However, it may necessitate an extension of approaches to green national accounting based on (implicit or explicit) assumptions of fixed technology. In common with Weitzman and Löfgren (1997) we have shown that – on the assumption that technological change is exogenous and costly (that is, not bought and sold) – a technological premium can be estimated as the (present) value of higher future output which is attributable to future productivity increases.

This empirical issue has a crucial bearing on the policy question as to the relative importance of the (net) accumulation of wealth and in sustaining future development prospects. The findings outlined in this chapter using cross-country estimates of (total factor) productivity growth available in the literature to some extent confirm the technological critique of green national accounting practice to date. Thus, if productivity growth is strong and leads to higher output being enjoyed 'for ever' then it is not surprising that estimates of technological premia can be large relative to the magnitude of estimates of changes in resource stocks and environmental liabilities. As we have shown, however, this is not always the case. If estimated rates of productivity growth are low or even negative, as appears to be the case for some countries, and if such a trend was likely to persist then, in accounting terms, this would be translated into low or negative estimates of technology premia to be added to measures of genuine saving. Put another way, the relative importance of technological change versus (net) wealth accumulation in determining sustainability prospects appears to need to be evaluated on a case-by-case basis.[8]

Yet the fact remains that to the extent that countries can manage to sustain a high level of productivity growth then green national accounting arguably offers little, in at least a number of instances, of empirical interest in terms of concerns about sustainable development. This is because even relatively crude estimates of the value of future growth attributable to technological change could more than offset any collateral liquidation of resource and environmental assets. Indeed, the only cloud on this otherwise clear horizon is whether development is also being financed by the liquidation of natural assets that can be thought of as 'critical' (for example, providing life support functions) (Hamilton et al., 1998). If so, then it is possible in theory that the loss of critical assets could be associated with substantial losses in welfare comparable to a technology premium, which is currently not accounted for. However, little or no reliable data exist at present to evaluate this claim in practice (although see Ekins et al., 2003).

In this chapter, we have added an additional note of caution. This is that it turns out to be of great importance whether or not technological change is characterized as an exogenous or an endogenous process. This point was made in principle by Pemberton and Ulph (2001) and our calculations have shown its importance in practice as well. Clearly, the key question is which of these two divergent theories describes more accurately the process whereby technological change comes into being?

On the one hand, it can be argued that the idea of endogenous technological progress – or more specifically the idea that economic resources diverted to R&D result in the creation of productivity-enhancing innovations – is the more convincing case. Indeed, this more detailed description of the innovation process is typically cited as the main contribution of the new growth theory.

On the other hand, the ability of less-technologically advanced countries to borrow or copy technologies from those countries that are more advanced technologically could potentially result in substantial sustained increases in productivity (Collins and Bosworth, 1996). Depending on how costly it is to acquire these technologies, then it might be that the exogenous technological change case is a more apt description for less advanced or less developed countries.

However, with respect to this last point, the evidence in Chapter 4 suggested that (per capita) wealth accumulation predicts (per capita) consumption growth less well in (mostly technologically advanced) OECD countries than in (mostly technologically disadvantaged) non-OECD countries. This might suggest evidence that, for some reason, this potential to enjoy 'exogenous' productivity improvements – in general – is not borne out in practice. As noted in Chapter 4, there are parallels here with discussion elsewhere in the literature on economic growth, particularly the debate on sources of economic growth in a number of East Asian economies. Thus a number of authors have sought to establish to what degree the recent economic successes of these countries can be explained by sacrifices of current consumption (that is, saving and investing for the future) or the adoption of existing and better technologies from elsewhere. An influential finding from Young (1995) is that the answer was the former (at least for South Korea, Singapore, Taiwan and Hong Kong). Collins and Bosworth

(1996) reach similar conclusions for a larger range of countries in this region (including Indonesia, Malaysia, the Philippines and Thailand).

For many, the magnitude of the adjustment that the alternative assumption of exogenous change would require to genuine saving seems unreasonably large in those cases where the estimated growth rate of total factor productivity is robustly positive. According to this view, a more cautious approach is that the likely value of a technological premium is closer to those values suggested by the endogenous case. Whether this is a judgement based largely on prudence rather than certainty about the balance of evidence is another matter. However, as outlined above, there does seem to be some empirical basis for not taking the rather dramatic policy implications of assuming wholly exogenous change at face value. Yet, neither should the reminder that these contributions have provided, about the importance of technological change for development prospects, be discounted. It could well be that reality in general lies between these two polar cases. That is, in terms of monitoring development prospects, it may be that even when all inputs – including R&D effort and so on – have been accounted for there is still some (presumably reduced) residual which should be translated into a technological premium. It is plain, however, that reconciling the divergence between the guidance that the two approaches give is a matter of some practical importance to measuring whether or not economies are on or off development paths which are sustainable.

NOTES

1. Dasgupta and Heal (1979) provided an early illustration of the importance of technological change as a necessary condition for making sustainability feasible because of the need to offset depreciation of produced assets.
2. For a logarithmic welfare function (that is, unitary elasticity of the marginal utility of consumption), it is straightforward to show that the steady-state growth rate of consumption in this model is given by $g - \beta r$, which leads to a not particularly stringent condition for sustainability: the rate of total factor productivity growth must be greater than the elasticity of output with respect to resource use times the pure rate of time preference.
3. As Weitzman (1997) shows, the social discount rate in the denominator in this expression, strictly speaking, should be adjusted for the growth rate of national product rather than the growth rate of TFP. However, we have in the illustrative calculations that are presented here only taken account of the latter.
4. Typically, data on g are numerated in terms of the contribution to the growth rate of GDP. In order to express this magnitude to GNP (as elsewhere in this volume), we have taken F_S to be GDP but have expressed the resulting dollar value of the technological premium as a percentage of GNP.
5. Appendix 8A.2 indicates the countries that make up each grouping.
6. See, for example, Jones (1998) for a review of more general ways of specifying this relationship between productivity growth and R&D, in particular in modelling the possibility of diminishing returns to R&D effort.

7. There will be positive growth in consumption (that is, sustainability) in this model if $\theta^* >$ βr, where θ^* is the steady-state value of the research effort.
8. While it is worth bearing in mind that estimates of productivity growth are themselves uncertain (Felipe, 1999) these data are perhaps no more uncertain than estimates of the value of changes in resource stocks and environmental liabilities.

APPENDIX 8A.1: HICKSIAN INCOME WITH EXOGENOUS TECHNICAL CHANGE

The model of exogenous technical change can serve as a useful example of the 'extended Hicksian' approach to measuring national income. For the variables defined in the body of the paper the current value Hamiltonian for the problem may be expressed as,

$$H^C = U + \gamma_1 \left(F - \delta K - C \right) + \gamma_2 \left(-R \right), \tag{8A.1}$$

where the γ_i are the shadow prices of produced assets and resource stocks. The static first order conditions for an optimum are given by,

$$\gamma_1 = U_C$$
$$\gamma_2 = U_C F_R$$

while the dynamic conditions are given by,

$$\frac{\dot{U}_C}{U_C} = r - \left(F_K - \delta \right) \text{ (the Ramsey rule),} \tag{8A.2}$$

$$\frac{\dot{F}_R}{F_R} = F_K - \delta \text{ (the Hotelling rule),} \tag{8A.3}$$

With these derivations in hand, we can define the current value Hamiltonian to be,

$$H^C = U + U_C \left(\dot{K} - F_R R \right). \tag{8A.4}$$

The rate of change of utility is given by,

$$\dot{U} = U_C \dot{C}$$
$$= U_C \left(\dot{F} - \ddot{K} - \delta \dot{K} \right)$$
$$= U_C \left(gF + F_K \dot{K} + F_R \dot{R} - \ddot{K} - \delta \dot{K} \right).$$

Defining net saving N to be

$$N \equiv \dot{K} - \delta K - F_R R,$$

it follows, by substituting expression (8A.3), that

$$\dot{U} = U_C \left(\left(F_K - \delta \right) N - \dot{N} + gF \right), \qquad (8A.5)$$

and therefore, by substituting expression (8A.2), that

$$\dot{H}^C = \dot{U} + \dot{U}_C N + U_C \dot{N} = U_C \left(rN + gF \right). \qquad (8A.6)$$

The present value Hamiltonian is given by,

$$H = \left(U + U_C N \right) e^{-rt},$$

which implies, substituting from expression (8A.6), that

$$\dot{H} = -re^{-rt}U + e^{-rt}U_C gF,$$

which has the solution,

$$H = r \int_t^\infty U e^{-rs} ds - \int_t^\infty U_C gFe^{-rs} ds.$$

From expression (8A.2) we know that,

$$U_{C_s} = U_C e^{r(s-t) - \int_t^s \left(F_K(\tau) - \delta \right) d\tau}.$$

From the definition of total wealth W it therefore follows that,

$$H^C = U + U_C N = rW - U_C g \int_t^\infty Fe^{-\int_t^s \left(F_K(\tau) - \delta \right) d\tau} ds.$$

Genuine saving G can therefore be defined as,

$$G \equiv N + g \int_t^\infty Fe^{-\int_t^s \left(F_K(\tau) - \delta \right) d\tau} ds.$$

The definition of total wealth implies that

$$\dot{W} = rW - U,$$

so that

$$U_c G = \dot{W}. \tag{8A.7}$$

Expression (8A.7) therefore implies that total wealth will decline on the optimum path if and only if the rate of genuine saving is negative at some point in time. The maximum amount of produced output that can be consumed at a point in time while leaving total wealth constant is therefore

$$NNP = C + G = C + \dot{K} - \delta K - F_R R + g \int_t^\infty Fe^{-\int_t^s (F_K(\tau) - \delta) d\tau} ds. \tag{8A.8}$$

This is the extended Hicksian definition of national income. If technological growth is truly exogenous then national income must include the present value of the future output growth that is attributable to technical change. The linkage to sustainability is provided by expression (8A.7).

APPENDIX 8A.2: LIST OF COUNTRIES IN SAMPLE

China

East Asia: Indonesia, Republic of Korea, Malaysia, Philippines, Singapore, Taiwan and Thailand

South Asia: Bangladesh, India, Myanmar, Pakistan, Sri Lanka

USA

Industrialized countries (excl. USA): Australia, Austria, Belgium, Canada, Denmark, Finland, France, Germany, Greece, Ireland, Italy, Japan, Netherlands, New Zealand, Norway, Portugal, Spain, Sweden, Switzerland, Turkey, United Kingdom

Latin America and Caribbean: Argentina, Bolivia, Brazil, Chile, Colombia, Costa Rica, Dominican Republic, Ecuador, El Salvador, Guatemala, Haiti, Honduras, Jamaica, Mexico, Nicaragua, Panama, Paraguay, Peru, Trinidad and Tobago, Uruguay, Venezuela

Middle East and North Africa: Algeria, Egypt, Iran, Israel, Jordan, Morocco, Tunisia

Sub-Saharan Africa: Cameroon, Congo, Dem. Rep. Côte d'Ivoire, Ethiopia, Ghana, Kenya, Madagascar, Malawi, Mali, Mauritius, Mozambique, Nigeria, Rwanda, Senegal, Sierra Leone, South Africa, Sudan, Tanzania, Uganda, Zambia, Zimbabwe.

Source: Collins and Bosworth (1996).

APPENDIX 8A.3

Table 8A.1   Data used in estimation of T

	TFP growth rate (g) (%)	Discount rate (δ) (%)	Gross domestic product (GDP) ($million) (1997)	Gross national product (GNP) ($million) (1997)
China	2.6	10.8	898243	882321
East Asia	1.1	7.5	279928	277252
Indonesia	0.8	10.1	215749	209440
Korea, Rep.	0.8	8.8	476486	473939
Malaysia	0.9	7.2	100168	84803
Philippines	−0.4	6.2	82343	85847
Thailand	1.8	10.6	140374	136715
South Asia	0.2	3.3	324461	321796
USA	0.8	3.4	8256500	8233800
Industrialized countries (excl. USA)	0.3	3.3	2069881	2083703
Latin America and Caribbean	0.8	2.5	472998	462503
Middle East and North Africa	−0.3	5.8	76721	75713
Sub-Saharan Africa	−0.6	2.6	77006	75043

Sources: Collins and Bosworth (1996); Hamilton (2000); World Bank (2003).

9. Resource price trends and prospects for development

INTRODUCTION[1]

This chapter explores empirically the effect of resource price trends on measures of income and saving. This is motivated by a basic intuition: if a country's terms of trade are improving and can be expected to continue to improve – an exporter of increasingly scarce natural resources would be an example – then this country should be able to increase its consumption without harming its future prospects. Its Hicksian income, in other words, should increase as a result of these favourable trends. Sustained unfavourable trends, by the same reasoning, should decrease Hicksian income. Vincent et al. (1997) made this intuition precise for the case of optimal resource extraction in the face of exogenous resource price changes. They then examined the case of Indonesia empirically.

In this chapter we offer several extensions to the work of Vincent et al. First, we develop an explicit model of income and saving in a small resource-exporting country where both resource prices and international interest rates vary exogenously. We then derive a precise formula for saving when resource prices grow at the exogenous international interest rate. Finally we present estimates of adjusted saving rates for roughly 100 countries by extrapolating significant resource price trends for a range of natural resources.

The model developed below extends, for non-autonomous economies, a result presented by Hamilton and Clemens (1999). We show that 'genuine' saving, suitably defined, just equals the change in social welfare (present value of utility) measured in dollars. This provides the link between resource price trends and development prospects.

THE SMALL RESOURCE EXPORTER

For a small exhaustible resource-exporting country, assume an exogenous path of international resource prices given by p and an exogenous path for international interest rates given by r (both implicitly time-varying). Non-renewable resource stock S is extracted at rate R. Extraction is assumed to cost $f(R)$, and to consist of domestically used quantity R_d and exported quantity R_x. Resources are the only exports. Utility U is a function of consumption C only, and production is given by function $F(K,R_d)$, where K is produced capital. For foreign assets A the following accounting identity holds,

$$\dot{A} = rA + pR_x - M, \tag{9.1}$$

where M is the value of imports. Supply and use are equated as follows:

$$F\left(K, R_d\right) + M = C + \dot{K} + f\left(R\right). \tag{9.2}$$

This does not resemble the usual identity for gross national product (consumption plus investment plus exports minus imports) because the only export is assumed to be the exhaustible resource, which is not a 'product' of the production function – it is extracted at cost $f(R_x)$ and sold at price p, and its chief effect is on the balance of foreign assets given by expression (9.1). The national accounting identity (9.2) says that the total potentially consumable quantity is $F + M$, and that this is divided optimally among consumption, investment and resource extraction expenditures.

For a fixed pure rate of time preference ρ, the optimal growth model for the exporting economy is therefore,

$$\max V = \int_t^\infty U\left(C(s)\right) e^{-\rho(s-t)} ds \text{ subject to:}$$
$$\dot{K} = F\left(K, R_d\right) + M - C - f\left(R\right)$$
$$\dot{S} = -R = -\left(R_d + R_x\right)$$
$$\dot{A} = rA + pR_x - M.$$

The control variables for this problem are C, R_x, R_d and M. The shadow prices in utils for produced capital, foreign assets and resource stocks are given by U_C, U_C and $U_C(F_{Rd} - f')$ respectively. Because produced capital and foreign assets have the same shadow price, the domestic price of resources F_{Rd} is constrained to be equal to the international resource price p. Defining the scarcity rent on resources to be $n \equiv F_{Rd} - f'$, the dynamic first order conditions for a maximum are given by,

$$\frac{\dot{U}_C}{U_C} = \rho - F_K \tag{9.3}$$

$$\frac{\dot{n}}{n} = F_K \tag{9.4}$$

These are the Ramsey and Hotelling rules respectively. The equality of the shadow prices for domestic and foreign assets implies that the domestic interest rate F_K must equal the international interest rate r.

Defining net saving $N \equiv \dot{K} + \dot{A} - nR$, the current value Hamiltonian is given by,

$$H^c = U + U_C N. \tag{9.5}$$

Applying expressions (9.3) and (9.4) and the equations for the rate of change of the state variables it follows that,

$$\dot{U} = U_C \left(F_K N - \dot{N} + \dot{r}A + \dot{p}R_x \right), \tag{9.6}$$

so that, from expressions (9.3) and (9.5),

$$\dot{H}^c = U_C \left(\rho N + \dot{r}A + \dot{p}R_x \right).$$

The rate of change of the present value Hamiltonian is therefore given by,

$$\dot{H} = -\rho H + e^{-\rho t} \dot{H}^c = -\rho e^{-\rho t} U + e^{-\rho t} U_C \left(\dot{r}A + \dot{p}R_x \right).$$

Integrating forward, the present value Hamiltonian may be expressed as,

$$H = \rho \int_t^\infty U\left(C(s) \right) e^{-\rho s} ds - \int_t^\infty U_C \left(C(s) \right) \left(\dot{r}(s) A(s) + \dot{p}(s) R_x(s) \right) e^{-\rho s} ds + \lim_{s \to \infty} H(s). \tag{9.7}$$

We assume that the latter limit equals 0. Recalling that U_C is implicitly $U_C(C(t))$, expression (9.3) can be used to express $U_C(C(s))$ as follows:

$$U_C \left(C(s) \right) = U_C \left(C(t) \right) e^{\rho(s-t) - \int_t^s F_K(\tau) d\tau} \quad \text{for } s > t. \tag{9.8}$$

Now expressions (9.7) and (9.8) can be combined to show that the current value Hamiltonian is given by,

$$H^c = \rho V - U_c \int_t^\infty \dot{r}(s)A(s)e^{-\int_t^s F_K(\tau)d\tau}ds - U_c \int_t^\infty \dot{p}(s)R_x(s)e^{-\int_t^s F_K(\tau)d\tau}ds.$$

(9.9)

Since $\dot{V} = \rho V - U$, it follows from expressions (9.5) and (9.9) that,

$$\dot{V} = U_c\left(N + \int_t^\infty \dot{r}(s)A(s)e^{-\int_t^s F_K(\tau)d\tau}ds + \int_t^\infty \dot{p}(s)R_x(s)e^{-\int_t^s F_K(\tau)d\tau}ds\right) \equiv U_c G.$$

(9.10)

Genuine saving G is defined as net saving plus the two present value of capital gains terms appearing in expression (9.10). V is social welfare. Genuine saving therefore equals the change in social welfare measured in dollars.

Note that a conventional measure of national income would be given by $C + N$, consumption plus net saving. From expression (9.6) we can derive the following relationship:

$$\dot{C} + \dot{N} = F_K N + \dot{r}A + \dot{p}R_x.$$

(9.11)

This expression says that growth in conventionally measured income is financed by the returns on net saving plus current capital gains on net foreign assets and resource exports.

We define *extended Hicksian income* (*NNI*) to be consumption of produced output plus genuine saving. This yields:

$$NNI = C + \dot{K} - nR + rA + pR_x - M$$
$$+ \int_t^\infty \dot{r}(s)A(s)e^{-\int_t^s F_K(\tau)d\tau}ds + \int_t^\infty \dot{p}(s)R_x(s)e^{-\int_t^s F_K(\tau)d\tau}ds. \quad (9.12)$$

The first part of this measure corresponds to standard national accounting practice: national income consists of consumption plus investment, minus resource depletion, plus the income on foreign assets, plus exports, minus imports. The final two terms reflect the effects of the exogenous paths followed by international interest rates and resource prices. Both measure the present value of capital gains – on foreign assets as a result of interest rate changes, and on resource exports as a result of price changes. On the optimal development path the latter two quantities are known; in doing real-world accounting we have to forecast these present values of capital gains terms, which is the subject of the next section of the chapter.

Some intuition into this measure of national income can be provided by considering the case where international interest rates are constant and resource prices are increasing over time. Under these circumstances the small resource exporter has an opportunity to benefit from the favourable trend in prices by increasing consumption and decreasing investment (but not so much as to drive genuine savings negative if sustainability is the goal – see below). The mere passage of time makes the exporter better off, because of the assumed rise in the price of its exports.

In fact, if international interest rates are constant and the resource price rises at the rate of interest, then it is straightforward to show that the present value of capital gains terms in expressions (9.10) and (9.11) reduce to,

$$\int_t^\infty \dot{r}(s)A(s)e^{-\int_t^s F_K(\tau)d\tau}ds + \int_t^\infty \dot{p}(s)R_x(s)e^{-\int_t^s F_K(\tau)d\tau}ds = rp\int_t^\infty R_x(s)ds = rpS_x,$$

where S_x is the stock of resource that will be exported. Genuine saving would then be measured as,

$$G = \dot{K} - nR + rA + pR_x - M + rpS_x = N + rpS_x.$$

To the ordinary expression for net saving (N), we therefore add the return on those resource assets slated for export.

In terms of the prospects for welfare in this economy, expression (9.10) is the critical result, relating the change in the present value of utility to the sum of net saving and the present values of the changes in the exogenous variables. For paths where genuine saving is everywhere positive, the present value of social welfare is everywhere increasing. If genuine saving is negative at a point in time, then utility must fall over some interval in the future – that is, the economy is unsustainable by Pezzey's (1989) definition.

Note that it is still possible for the resource-exporting economy to optimally deplete its resource even in the face of projected decreases in resource prices. The opinion is often expressed that if resource prices are falling, the best thing for a resource exporter to do is to extract the resource as quickly as possible and invest the rents in other assets. This is surely sub-optimal if the marginal cost of extraction curve is sufficiently upward sloping – in this case the Hotelling rule can still be enforced by driving marginal costs down at a sufficient rate relative to the declining price.

Measured depletion and income would need to reflect the declining price path as indicated by expressions (9.10) and (9.12).

With this as the theoretical background, we now turn to the practical question of measuring the effects of exogenous price change for resource-exporting countries.

METHODOLOGY OF CALCULATION

While the formal model suggests that genuine saving should be adjusted to reflect capital gains on resource exports, below we calculate adjustments reflecting total resource extraction and not just exports. For large countries with high rates of use of domestic natural resources, therefore, this may produce results which diverge from theory.[2]

Expression (9.10) contains two terms linked to exogenous trends, one associated with movements in international interest rates, the other with resource prices. Since there is no reason to expect a long-run trend in interest rates, this term will be assumed to be zero in what follows. The term in resource prices is measured in discrete time as follows:

$$\sum_{j=0}^{N-1} R_{s0} P_{s0} \cdot \frac{\dot{p}_s}{p_s} \cdot \frac{\left(1 + \frac{\dot{p}_s}{p_s}\right)^j}{\left(1 + \delta\right)^j}, \text{ where,}$$

$$(9.13)$$

p_{s0} is the base period price of resource s;

$\dot{p}_s/p_s$ is the growth rate of the price of resource s (assumed to be constant);
R_{s0} is the total quantity of resource extracted (assumed to be constant to the point of exhaustion);
δ is the social discount rate;
N is the number of years to resource exhaustion.

Current dollar price and quantity data were derived from the World Bank's adjusted net (genuine) saving data base, described in World Bank (2002b). World prices were deflated using the manufacturers unit value (MUV) index. This is a unit value index (in US dollars) of manufactures exported from the G-5 countries (France, Germany, Japan, the United Kingdom and the United States) weighted proportionally to the countries' exports to developing countries.

Resource price growth rates were estimated by regressing real resource prices against time from 1970 to 1999, the period covered by the World

Bank's genuine saving database. The estimated growth rates are reported in Table 9.1. For the purposes of projecting these growth rates into the future, we chose only those resources for which the price trend is significant at 10 per cent or better, which, notably, excludes oil from the analysis below – our results are clearly contingent on the choice of period for the trend analysis.

Table 9.1   Price trend coefficients, 1970–99

	Estimated growth rate (%)	t statistic
Bauxite	–2.6 **	–6.4
Copper	–2.3 **	–5.5
Iron	–1.8 **	–8.1
Lead	–2.0 **	–4.2
Nickel	–1.4 **	–2.7
Phosphate	–1.8 **	–2.7
Tin	–4.8 **	–6.9
Gold	1.4 *	1.8
Silver	–2.6 **	–2.9
Zinc	–0.8 *	–1.9
Industrial diamond	–2.7	–0.8
Oil	0.3	0.3
Hard coal	–1.4 **	–2.8
Soft coal	–1.4 **	–2.8
Gas	–0.7	–1.1
Roundwood:		
Non coniferous – tropical	1.3 ·	–0.7
Non coniferous – other	–1.2	1.8
Coniferous	–3.7 **	3.5

Notes: **: significant at 5%; *: significant at 10%.

Current reserves and extraction rates are used to calculate the expected life of the resource. Reserves and extraction data were obtained from several sources:

- *Minerals*: USGS (2001a,b) reserves data were used, defined as those known resources which could be economically extracted at time of determination.
- *Energy*: Reserves data were taken from British Petroleum (2001), defined as those quantities that geological and engineering information

indicates with reasonable certainty can be recovered in the future from known deposits under *existing* economic and operating conditions. Production data for soft coal is measured as total lignite production taken from IEA (2001) and UNCTAD (2001). Hard coal production data is reported as an aggregate of steam and coking coal, obtained from IEA (2001) and UNCTAD (2001).

*   *Forests*: Since resource lives are potentially infinite, these were capped at 50 years in the calculation of expression (9.13) – this serves to 'level the playing field' between exhaustible and renewable resources (see next paragraph).

Many countries have mineral and energy reserves in excess of 100 years production at current rates. Given the inherent uncertainties about how valuable these resources will be in the future, we capped large resource reserves at 50 years, so that $N \leq 49$ in expression (9.13). Where reserves data are missing, but production data are available, it was assumed that reserves were sufficient to support 15 years production (this is roughly the time frame over which resource firms write off their capital investments).

Finally, a choice of social discount rate is required in the calculation of expression (9.13). Estimates of social discount rates in industrial countries range from 2–4 per cent (Pearce and Ulph, 1999; and Zerbe and Dively, 1994). For fast-growing developing countries rates may be as high as 7–9 per cent and for the slowest growing economies near zero (World Bank, 1997). We use a uniform rate of 4 per cent to facilitate cross-country comparisons, but it is clear that in analysing any individual country it would be more appropriate to use a country-specific social discount rate (see, for example, Chapter 7).

RESULTS

Appendix 9A.1 reports the country-level results on the present value of capital gains and adjustments to genuine saving, sorted in increasing order of present value. These results reflect the particular countries where there is extraction of natural resources which have significant price trends. We first examine the aggregate results.

At aggregate level, by income or region, the present value of capital gains from future world price changes has a negative effect on savings, as shown in tables 9.2 and 9.3. This reflects, of course, the fact that only gold has had a significant positive price trend over the 30 year historical period, as seen in Table 9.1. The adjustments to national income and savings from resource price trends are substantial, 0.4 per cent of GNI or more in all regions except the Middle East and North Africa (recall that oil prices did not have a significant trend), and all income groups except high income. The largest effects are seen in Eastern Europe and Central Asia and in lower middle income countries.

Table 9.2   Impact of exogenous changes in world prices on regional genuine savings rates, 1999

	PV of capital gains (% GNI)	Genuine savings (% GNI)	Adjusted genuine savings (% GNI)
Latin America and the Caribbean	–0.4	6.8	6.4
South Asia	–0.6	11.7	11.1
East Asia Pacific	–0.7	22.1	21.4
Eastern Europe and Central Asia	–1.4	3.4	2.0
Middle East and North Africa	–0.1	–3.3	–3.4
Sub-Saharan Africa	–0.5	0.1	–0.4

Table 9.3   Impact of exogenous changes in world prices on income group genuine savings rates, 1999

	PV of capital gains (% GNI)	Genuine savings (% GNI)	Adjusted genuine savings (% GNI)
Low income	–0.5	5.6	5.1
Lower middle	–0.9	14.9	14.0
Upper middle income	–0.4	9.9	9.5
High income	–0.1	12.7	12.6

The country-level results in Appendix 9A.1 show that 22 countries had negative adjustments of more than 1 per cent of GNI when resource price trends are taken into account. These include nine countries in Eastern Europe and Central Asia, five in Sub-Saharan Africa, two each in Latin America and the Caribbean and East Asia, one in Middle East and North Africa, and three OECD countries – Australia, New Zealand and Finland. Two countries, Uzbekistan and the Kyrgyz Republic, had positive adjustments of over 1 per cent of GNI.

ISSUES

The assumption in the foregoing that all countries are price-takers deserves a closer look, since there may be resource markets where countries alone or in collusion have pricing power. We therefore calculate the Hirschman-Herfindahl Index (HHI),[3] a measure of market concentration, for each resource commodity. Appendix 9A.2 displays those countries which command a market share in excess of 10 per cent of any given natural resource, as well as the HHI for each commodity. As this appendix shows, most of the resource markets are moderately concentrated, with tin and soft coal being highly concentrated. Of the countries in Appendix 9A.1 having a present value of capital gains greater than 1 per cent of GNI, it seems likely that Australia and Chile (at least) have considerable market power.

If market power were exercised with respect to particular resources, then resource prices would effectively be endogenized by a welfare-maximizing resource exporter. For the theoretical model presented earlier, this would imply that the terms representing exogenous price changes (terms in $\dot{p}$) would disappear; empirically, this would imply no adjustment for future price trends.

Diamonds were excluded from the analysis owing to data availability issues and the lack of free market prices. However, it should be noted that this may misrepresent the true genuine savings rate in countries where diamonds are an important resource, most significantly in Angola, Botswana, Congo (DR), Namibia, Russian Federation and South Africa.

The lack of significant price trends for crude petroleum over the 30-year span examined in this chapter clearly has a major impact on the empirical results. The preponderance of oil extraction in many 'oil states' suggests that any *expected* price trend for crude petroleum should figure prominently in the analysis of income and saving in these countries.

CONCLUSIONS

It should be obvious that extrapolating resource prices for 50 years into the future, based on simple historical regressions, is not a very precise science. The empirical results presented here are therefore no more than indicative of the potential impacts of capital gains on saving and income. It is striking, nonetheless, that the long-run decline in most resource prices observed in the later twentieth century, when extrapolated into the future, leads to significant reductions in 'adjusted' saving in over 20 countries.

The formal model suggests how future capital gains and losses should be accounted in assessments of national income and saving. For countries with significant resource dependence, the empirical results suggest that future growth rates in natural resource prices can have a tangible impact on current measures of genuine saving, with consequent effects on development prospects. In measuring income and genuine saving in resource-dependent economies, therefore, the analysis should consider the impact of likely trends in future resource prices.

NOTES

1. This chapter is based on Hamilton and Bolt (2004).
2. Because governments generally tax resource extraction, we have greater confidence in the extraction data than in the export data.
3. The HHI is calculated by summing the squares of the market shares (per cent) of all players in the market. Unconcentrated markets have an HHI less than 1000; HHIs in excess of 1800 indicate high concentration.

APPENDIX 9A.1

Table 9A.1   *Impact of exogenous resource price changes on savings rates,*
(% GNI) 1999

Country	PV of capital gains (% GNI)	Genuine saving (% GNI)	Adjusted genuine saving (% GNI)
Mauritania	−10.0	0.5	−9.5
Mongolia	−5.5	–	–
Zambia	−5.0	–	–
Kazakhstan	−4.8	−14.9	−19.7
Guinea	−3.6	7.3	3.7
Ukraine	−3.6	–	–
Chile	−3.4	10.3	6.8
Latvia	−3.2	12.1	8.9
Zimbabwe	−3.0	–	–
Russian Federation	−2.5	−8.2	−10.6
Estonia	−2.4	9.1	6.7
Jamaica	−1.4	14.2	12.8
Poland	−1.2	13.0	11.8
China	−1.2	27.4	26.2
Australia	−1.1	6.5	5.4
Togo	−1.1	5.1	4.0
Czech Republic	−1.0	18.0	17.0
Bulgaria	−1.0	2.4	1.4
Yugoslavia, FR (Serb./Mont.)	−1.0	–	–
Morocco	−1.0	17.1	16.1
New Zealand	−1.0	8.4	7.4
Finland	−1.0	15.6	14.6
Jordan	−0.9	18.1	17.2
Peru	−0.9	8.6	7.7
Canada	−0.9	11.6	10.7
Botswana	−0.9	7.2	6.4
South Africa	−0.8	5.3	4.5
India	−0.7	12.8	12.0
Lao PDR	−0.7	–	–
Sweden	−0.7	13.9	13.2
Romania	−0.6	3.2	2.7
Brazil	−0.6	8.0	7.5
Honduras	−0.5	25.6	25.0

Country	PV of capital gains (% GNI)	Genuine saving (% GNI)	Adjusted genuine saving (% GNI)
Lithuania	–0.5	5.7	5.2
Bolivia	–0.5	4.4	3.9
Indonesia	–0.5	2.5	2.0
Macedonia, FYR	–0.4	–	–
Colombia	–0.4	–1.9	–2.3
Slovak Republic	–0.4	18.4	18.1
Senegal	–0.4	7.6	7.2
Congo, Dem. Rep.	–0.3	–	–
Belarus	–0.3	16.2	15.9
Tunisia	–0.3	19.0	18.8
Vietnam	–0.2	14.5	14.2
Namibia	–0.2	22.3	22.1
Kenya	–0.2	10.2	10.0
Dominican Republic	–0.2	18.7	18.5
United States	–0.2	9.8	9.7
Burundi	–0.2	–1.4	–1.6
Slovenia	–0.2	17.1	16.9
Venezuela	–0.2	1.1	0.9
Armenia	–0.2	–8.3	–8.4
Syrian Arab Republic	–0.2	–18.9	–19.1
Tanzania	–0.2	3.2	3.1
Malawi	–0.2	–9.2	–9.3
Portugal	–0.2	8.7	8.6
Turkey	–0.1	18.7	18.5
Greece	–0.1	12.5	12.4
Norway	–0.1	17.8	17.6
Austria	–0.1	11.5	11.4
Mexico	–0.1	10.5	10.4
Hungary	–0.1	16.1	16.0
Ireland	–0.1	22.1	22.0
Ecuador	–0.1	4.9	4.8
Sierra Leone	–0.1	–	–
Iran, Islamic Rep.	–0.1	–11.0	–11.1
Uganda	–0.1	3.4	3.3
Georgia	–0.1	–8.5	–8.6
Madagascar	–0.1	1.0	0.9
Uruguay	–0.1	3.9	3.8
Croatia	–0.1	–	–

Table 9A.1 (continued)

Country	PV of capital gains (% GNI)	Genuine saving (% GNI)	Adjusted genuine saving (% GNI)
Germany	–0.1	10.5	10.4
Algeria	–0.1	–	–
Haiti	–0.1	–	–
Guatemala	–0.1	1.5	1.5
Rwanda	–0.1	3.0	2.9
Bosnia and Herzegovina	–0.1	–	–
Spain	–0.1	14.3	14.2
Argentina	–0.1	4.3	4.2
Israel	–0.1	7.3	7.3
Nicaragua	0.1	2.0	2.1
Ethiopia	0.1	–11.1	–11.1
Sudan	0.1	–8.7	–8.6
Ghana	0.4	3.4	3.8
Tajikistan	0.4	7.7	8.1
Papua New Guinea	0.5	–	–
Uzbekistan	1.8	–17.7	–15.9
Kyrgyz Republic	3.6	–4.0	–0.4

APPENDIX 9A.2

Table A9.2   Degree of market concentration

Countries with market share > 10%	
Bauxite [HHI: 1750]	Australia (35) Zimbabwe (15) Guinea (11)
Nickel [HHI: 1427]	Russian Federation (25) Canada (21) Australia (14)
Iron [HHI: 1205]	Brazil (23) Australia (17) China (11)
Zinc [HHI: 959]	United States (10) Peru (11) China (17) Canada (14) Australia (14)
Lead [HHI: 1235]	Australia (20) China (19) United States (16)
Phosphate [HHI: 1674]	United States (31) China (18) Morocco (17)
Tin [HHI: 2203]	China (36) Indonesia (25) Peru (12)
Gold [HHI: 965]	United States (15) South Africa (19) Australia (13)
Silver [HHI: 859]	Mexico (16) Peru (12) United States (13)
Copper [HHI: 1557]	Chile (35) United States (13)
Hard coal [HHI: 1492]	Australia (31) South Africa (12) Indonesia (10) United States (10)
Soft coal [HHI: 5071]	Czech Republic (64) Russia (32)
Coniferous industrial roundwood [HHI: 1672]	New Zealand (10) Russian Federation (34) United States (17)

Note: HHI – Hirschman-Herfindahl Index.

10. International flows of resource rents

INTRODUCTION

The role that international trade plays in *measuring* sustainable development has come under recent scrutiny, reflecting in part the wider and diverse debate about trade and sustainability. For example, by relaxing domestic natural resource constraints it has been argued that international trade allows any particular country to deplete natural assets abroad by importing its natural resource requirements. While the onus is on resource-extracting countries to make provision for the loss of domestic natural assets whether for export or not, some importing countries have expressed interest in measuring their derived demand for the depletion of resources elsewhere. For both selfish and altruistic reasons, such information may be of particular interest where an exporter is believed to be on an unsustainable path.

In this chapter, we examine international resource flows using an Input/ Output framework that is akin to an 'ecological balance of payments' analysis. This framework allows us to calculate the derived demand for resources in the country of final use. The empirical section of this chapter applies this model to data on global trade and natural resource depletion in 1980, 1985 and 1990. Our results provide a quantitative assessment of the significance of imports of resources – direct and indirect – required by, say, Japan, the United States and the European Union. These results can also be disaggregated to permit an examination of trade relations vis-à-vis individual resource exporting countries. It is interesting to note that a number of these resource exporters appear to be unsustainable at least on the basis of the criterion that the savings rate net of asset consumption (that is, genuine savings) should not be negative. These findings, in turn, could form the basis of policies to assist exporters in adopting prudent resource and public investment policies.

INTERNATIONAL TRADE AND SUSTAINABLE DEVELOPMENT

As argued in chapters 1 and 2, in order to achieve sustainability, a country that is liquidating its natural assets must set aside sufficient economic resources to finance investment in other forms of wealth (so that substitutions of, for example, natural and produced assets are possible). This has led to a focus on adjusted net savings measures that account for the depletion of natural resources and environmental damage.

In this chapter we focus only on one particular criticism of genuine savings: that it does not distinguish between those natural resources that are for export and those that are not. Chapter 9 offered one response to this criticism. In this current chapter, our starting point is that view exemplified by Martinez-Alier (1995) that estimates of genuine saving appear to suggest that unsustainable countries tend to be located in the developing world. Many developing countries are highly dependent on resource extraction activities and the depletion of these assets often means that high levels of savings need to be generated if aggregate real wealth is not to be run down. Given that these resources are often traded with developed countries, a relevant question is whether this resource trade affects sustainability and its measurement. Put another way, could international trade lead countries down an unsustainable path, and could indicators such as genuine savings mask this?[1]

The specific question raised by Martinez-Alier (1995) is whether an 'ecological balance of payments' analysis would show that the USA and Japan, which exhibited positive genuine savings in the analysis of Pearce and Atkinson (1993) (and World Bank, 1997), were actually unsustainable when global resource flows are taken into account. A more formal analysis is proposed by Klepper and Stähler (1998) who show that a resource importer, which perhaps is leaving its own resources intact as a result of a (unilateral) restriction on domestic uses, could be characterized as 'buying' sustainability at the expense of a resource exporter. In terms of measurement, by modelling the total value of resource trade between countries, one response to this debate might be that – in the genuine savings framework – it is the savings of a resource importer that should be debited for use of a resource (Proops et al., 1999; Proops and Atkinson, 1998; Bailey and Clarke, 2000). However, it is unclear why the savings rate of a resource-importing country should be reduced to reflect the depreciation of an asset (the resource stock of the exporting country) that does not belong to it, so the logic of the question may be faulted. Strong demand for the natural resources of an exporting country could plausibly lead such a country down an unsustainable path, but only if its own policies are deficient – for instance, if resource royalties are not captured, resource tenure is insecure or resource rents are not invested in other assets.

In the end it is the resource and public investment policies of the resource exporters that determines whether or not they are on a sustainable path. Nevertheless, developed countries are to a large extent reliant on foreign resources to support their domestic economies and, moreover, several of these countries – for example, the Netherlands – have expressed concern over their demand for resource depletion in other countries. A variety of motivations underlie this concern, such as externalities associated with resource extraction (Bosch and Ensing, 1996). More broadly, resource-importing (developed) countries could be concerned about unsustainable behaviour on the part of resource-exporting (developing) countries for reasons both of self-interest and altruism.

From a purely self-interested point of view, importers may be concerned about the security and stability of supply of natural resources. If important sectors of their economies are dependent on resource imports, then supply shocks and price shocks are potentially quite damaging. Unsustainable behaviour on the part of resource exporters – overly rapid depletion of sub-soil resources, for instance – creates risks for importers. Tracing the flows of natural resources in international trade and measuring the degree of dependence on individual countries or regions may therefore be in the interest of developed countries.

From a more altruistic viewpoint, governments in developed countries provide considerable amounts of finance on concessional terms to aid the development of poorer countries. Since unsustainable behaviour is in essence the consumption of assets, countries providing development assistance are increasingly concerned about the effectiveness of this assistance when aid recipients are on an unsustainable path – these types of concerns underlie the 'greening' of development finance institutions such as the World Bank.

Identifying resource trade linkages to particular developing countries or regions may be of interest to wealthier nations in targeting their development assistance, particularly 'policy-based' loans or grants with conditionality aimed at policy reform. In other words, a means of informing these concerns would be to provide an analysis of the extent to which economic activity in (primarily) developed economies is dependent on resource imports from (primarily) developing countries. This is analogous to an 'ecological balance of payments' analysis. However, it is important to note that while this could highlight the policy failures of resource exporters, we do not ascribe 'responsibility' for this to importers in the sense of debiting (explicitly or implicitly) a country's savings rate for the resources that it imports.

There are a number of concepts and analytical approaches that could be used in this respect to construct this ecological balance of payments analysis.

Rees and Wackernagel (1994) argue that the impacts of economic activity of an individual country can be viewed in terms of the needs of its population relative to the country's carrying capacity or available land. This is the so-called 'ecological footprint': the extent to which a particular country (or region) is reliant on resources from elsewhere to support domestic economic activity. These needs can be expressed in a number of ways, such as the land required to satisfy nutritional requirements or by converting fossil energy into land required to grow the equivalent biofuel. If this required area is larger than the area actually available to that country, then in this sense the country has an ecological deficit. Analysing 51 countries, Wackernagel et al. (2000) find that most developed countries have significant deficits (although see, for a detailed critique of footprints approach, van Kooten and Bulte, 2000).

An alternative approach is suggested by Input/Output (I/O) analysis (see Miller and Blair, 1985; Førsund, 1985). For example, Pedersen (1993) has used an I/O framework to analyse net exports of transboundary ('acid rain') pollution in Denmark vis-à-vis the rest of the world. Similarly, Young (1996) examines the relative pollution intensity of traded (export-oriented) sectors and non-traded sectors in the Brazilian economy. An analogous framework could be used to construct an ecological balance of payments that quantifies resource trade interdependencies between countries. It should be noted that this is not the only means of carrying out this analysis. A somewhat different approach is adopted by Bailey and Clarke (2000) using a computable general equilibrium framework to model and forecast sustainability prospects in the world economy taking into account resource trade between major trading blocs.

A useful feature of I/O analysis is that not only can direct flows of resources be examined but also those indirect flows. For example, although Japan imports timber resources from Indonesia or Malaysia, a significant portion of these resources could be embodied in produced goods for subsequent export to another country, say the USA. A reasonable definition – in terms of where the resource ultimately ends up satisfying (domestic) final demand – suggests that the 'derived demand' for this resource depletion be attributed to the USA. In the remainder of this chapter, we develop an analytical approach based on I/O analysis that permits the calculation of this derived demand. This is defined as direct and indirect flows of resources in international trade and thereby extends the methods presented in Proops and Atkinson (1998) and Proops et al. (1999).

FRAMEWORK FOR ANALYSING FLOWS OF RESOURCES IN INTERNATIONAL TRADE

We wish to attribute resource depletion to the country where it eventually goes to support (domestic) final demand. Input/Output analysis captures these interactions in two ways. Firstly, there are *direct* exports of domestically extracted resources such as crude oil. This is typically what is conceived of as 'resource trade'. Secondly, an additional aspect to trade is *indirect* flows whereby resources are embodied in produced goods destined for markets abroad. As an example, country *j* might directly import resources from country *i*, which it then uses as an input in the production of traded goods (for example, manufactures) for subsequent export to country *k*. In this instance, the Input/Output framework will attribute the resource depletion not to country *j* but to country *k*.

We seek to calculate the derived demand for resources in the country of final use: that is, trace resource depletion (that is, current resource rents) from the country of extraction to the country where the resource was actually 'consumed'. Our framework for calculating these direct and indirect flows of resources is set out below but first, it is useful to define two indicators that elucidate these issues:

1. We denote by N the (total) *domestic resource depletion* required to support gross national product (Y). This is simply the value of depletion of domestically extracted resources familiar in green national accounting: that is, the product of the unit resource rent and quantity of resources extracted or harvested. It is useful to note that N has two components: domestic extracted resources that are consumed domestically and (direct) export of resources abroad.
2. The second measure N* is the *global resource consumption* required to support domestic final demand (that is, consumption plus investment). N* excludes the domestic resources used to produce exports, and includes all of the foreign resources consumed in making up some portion of domestic final demand.

Next we define [N-N*]. This is a summary indicator of the ecological balance of payments. A negative dollar value of [N-N*] indicates that a country's use or consumption of global resources to support its own domestic final demand is *less* than the total resources it uses (that is, depletes) to support its GNP. Put more simply, [N-N*]<0 indicates that a country is a net consumer of global resources. Examples of countries that are likely to have a negative dollar value of [N-N*] are Japan and the United States. Conversely, [N-N*]>0 indicates that a country is a net producer of global resources. Examples of these countries are likely to be resource-abundant economies such as Indonesia. More generally, the calculation of [N-N*] across countries permits the quantification of the degree to which the developed world is reliant on the resources of developing countries to support their domestic economies.

ACCOUNTING FRAMEWORK

In order to quantify these trade interactions we consider a simple two-country global economy. The basic accounting identities for these countries are:

$$X_{12} - X_{21} + C_1 + I_1 = Y_1$$
$$X_{21} - X_{12} + C_2 + I_2 = Y_2 \tag{10.1}$$

where, Y_i is country i's total output (or GNP); C_i is consumption in country i; I_i is investment in country i and; X_{ij} are the exports from country i to country j.

Relating the imports into each country to the GNP of that country, we define the following import coefficient (of country j):

$$q_{ij} \equiv \frac{X_{ij}}{Y_j}.$$

So, we can write:

$$X_{ij} = q_{ij} Y_j. \tag{10.2}$$

Substituting for X_{ij} in the above accounting identities and rewriting in matrix form we obtain,

$$\begin{pmatrix} -q_{21} & q_{12} \\ q_{21} & -q_{12} \end{pmatrix} \begin{pmatrix} Y_1 \\ Y_2 \end{pmatrix} + \begin{pmatrix} C_1 + I_1 \\ C_2 + I_2 \end{pmatrix} = \begin{pmatrix} Y_1 \\ Y_2 \end{pmatrix}. \tag{10.3}$$

This result can be generalized to several countries giving,

$$q_{ij} = \begin{bmatrix} \dfrac{X_{ij}}{Y_j}, & i \neq j \\ \dfrac{-\sum_k X_{kj}}{Y_j}, & i = j \end{bmatrix}$$

Defining a matrix of import coefficients (**Q**), the above expression means that all non-diagonal elements of **Q** describe imports to country j from each country i (X_{ij}) expressed as a proportion of j's gross national product (Y_j). The diagonal elements of $\mathbf{Q}$ are the (negative) sum of import coefficients for each country j vis-à-vis its trading partners in other countries. This generalization to several countries, permits the calculation of Y in each country based on the domestic final demand (C + I) in all countries. We can rewrite the output accounting identity in expression (10.3) in condensed matrix form.

$$\mathbf{Qy} + (\mathbf{c} + \mathbf{i}) = \mathbf{y}. \tag{10.4}$$

This can be reorganized to give (where $\mathbf{I}$ is the unit matrix):

$$(\mathbf{c} + \mathbf{i}) = (\mathbf{I} - \mathbf{Q})\mathbf{y}. \tag{10.5}$$

Solving expression (10.5) for $\mathbf{y}$, by matrix inversion, gives:

$$\mathbf{y} = (\mathbf{I} - \mathbf{Q})^{-1}(\mathbf{c} + \mathbf{i}) \tag{10.6}$$

Next we define a resource depletion vector $-\mathbf{n}$ where for each country i, n_i is defined as the share of all its resources in gross national product. This can be written as the sum of the products of, p_{im}, the resource rent on resource m of the country's s resources and R_{im}, the extraction rate for resource m of the country's s resources expressed as a proportion of Y_i:

$$n_i = \frac{\sum\limits_{m=s}^{s} p_{im} R_{im}}{Y_i}$$

Then the depletion of total domestic resources required to support Y is given by:

$$\mathbf{N} = \hat{\mathbf{n}}'(\mathbf{I} - \mathbf{Q})^{-1}(\mathbf{c} + \mathbf{i}) \tag{10.7}$$

Where the 'hat' notation indicates that the entries in $\hat{\mathbf{n}}$ are the diagonal elements of otherwise null matrices. $\mathbf{N}$ is a column matrix the elements of which indicate for each country i the (total) *domestic resource depletion* required to support gross national product (Y_i). Recall that this is the same as the dollar value of depletion of domestically extracted resources: that is, the product of the unit resource rent and quantity of resources extracted or harvested.

An alternative expression allows the calculation of the total direct and indirect consumption of global resources required to support the domestic final demand of each country:

$$\mathbf{N}^* = \mathbf{n}(\mathbf{I} - \mathbf{Q})^{-1}(\mathbf{c} \,\hat{+}\, \mathbf{i})$$

$$(10.8)$$

Recall that any country's N* indicates the dollar value of the *global resource consumption* required to support domestic final demand (that is, consumption plus investment). In contrast to N above, N* *excludes* the domestic resources used to produce a country's exports and *includes* all of the foreign resources that the country consumes (in support of its domestic final demand). The calculation of [N-N*] is our summary indicator of an 'ecological balance of payments', in that it measures *net* consumption of global resources.[2] Before we proceed to our main empirical application, we briefly illustrate a numerical application of the framework using a relatively simple three-country example.

AN EXAMPLE USING THE ACCOUNTING FRAMEWORK

The following example is adapted from Proops and Atkinson (1998) and involves three countries. Table 10.1 illustrates the basic data required to estimate an ecological balance of payments for these three countries as indicated by the value of [N-N*].

Table 10.1   Basic data for 3-country example

Country	1	2	3	Exports	C + I	Y
1	0	2	4	6	15	15
2	2	0	20	22	45	50
3	4	15	0	19	105	100
Imports	6	15	24			
n	0.33	0.50	0.10			

From Table 10.1 it can be seen that countries 1 and 2 are resource rich in that the share of resources in gross national product (n_j) is 33 per cent and 50 per cent respectively. Country 3 is less resource rich (that is, its resources

account for 10 per cent of its GNP). However, this country has the highest
level of economy activity of the three and it is plausible that this is supported
by the import of resources from abroad. The starting point for quantifying
this are the data on trade flows and values of resource and gross national
product and domestic final demand in each country.

*Table 10.2   The **Q** and (**I**–**Q**)⁻¹ matrices for 3-country example*

Q matrix			(**I**–**Q**)⁻¹ matrix		
–0.400	0.040	0.040	0.722	0.028	0.028
0.133	–0.340	0.200	0.099	0.778	0.129
0.267	0.300	–0.240	0.179	0.194	0.844

Table 10.2 shows the matrix of trade coefficients (**Q**) and the Leontief
inverse (**I** – **Q**)⁻¹. Note that the non-diagonal elements of **Q** are individual
import coefficients for each country vis-à-vis the countries with which it
trades. For example, in column 1, the entry 0.267 corresponds to the value
of imports to country 1 from country 3 expressed as proportion of country
1's GNP (that is, 4/15). Immediately above that the entry 0.133 corresponds
to the value of imports to country 1 from country 2 (again) expressed as
proportion of country 1's GNP (that is, 2/15). Finally, the first entry in
column 1 (that is, one of the diagonal elements of **Q**) is the (negative) sum
of these import coefficients: that is, –[0.133 + 0.267] = 0.400.

Combining the information in Tables 10.1 and 10.2, the values of N and
N* can be calculated for each country using expressions (10.7) and (10.8)
respectively (see Table 10.3).

Table 10.3   Ecological balance of payments [N-N] for 3-country example*

N	N*	[N-N*]
5.0	4.6	0.4
25.0	18.8	6.2
10.0	16.6	–6.6

Not surprisingly, countries 1 and 2 are net exporters of resources on the
basis of a positive estimate of [N-N*]. Thus in turn to satisfy domestic final
demand, country 3 – on balance – consumes 6.6 units of natural resources
from the 'rest of the world'.

EMPIRICAL APPLICATION: GLOBAL TRADING ECONOMY

Our empirical analysis describes an ecological balance of payments for the global trading economy in 1980, 1985 and 1990. This is made up of 95 individual countries (OECD – 23; (Former) Soviet Union and Eastern Europe – 8; Africa – 23; Central and South America – 18; Middle East – 11; Asia – 11; Oceania – 1). The remaining trading blocs are residual regions, namely: the 'Rest of Africa', the 'Rest of Central and South America', the 'Rest of Asia' and the 'Rest of Oceania'. Trade flows data are taken from OECD (1994) and IMF (various). These data describe trade flows (that is, the value of imports and exports) between different countries in the global trading economy. For each country, therefore, data indicating the value of its imports from each of its trading partners are described (for example, X_{ij}). Arranging these import data for all 95 countries (plus residual regions) provides the basis for calculating import coefficients which allows the construction of an I/O table (**Q**) based on the values of import coefficients (q_{ij}) as described in the previous section. Data on the depletion of commercial natural resources and gross national product for each country (Y_i) are taken from World Bank (1997). The resource data consist of depletion values for crude oil, timber, zinc, iron ore, phosphate rock, bauxite, copper, tin, lead, nickel, gold and silver. Hence, while our analysis cannot be claimed to be a full ecological balance of payments – in that we only analyse a subset of natural assets – the data cover relatively comprehensively (but not exhaustively) commercial natural assets.

Net Consumption of Global Resources

Figure 10.1 illustrates net consumption of global resources [N-N*] by region for the year 1985. What this indicates is whether or not a particular region is either: (i) a net producer of global resources, that is, [N-N*]>0, or; (ii) is a net consumer of global resources, that is, [N-N*]<0. For example, as is expected, OECD countries are, on average, net consumers of global resources. It can also be seen that Sub-Saharan Africa (SSA) is a net producer of resources – although this is clearly not as pronounced as for the Middle East and North Africa (MENA) (which represents the big oil exporters). The SSA case mainly reflects resource exports of oil (Nigeria, Congo, Cameroon and Zaire[3]), metals (Zaire and Zambia) and timber (Cameroon). Latin America (LAM) is a net producer of resources reflecting, to some extent, oil extraction in Venezuela, Mexico and Ecuador.

Figure 10.2 disaggregates the OECD region and in doing so reveals that much of its consumption is accounted for by the European Union (EU)

Wealth, welfare and sustainability

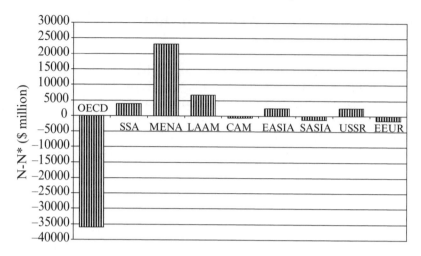

Figure 10.1   Net consumption of global resources [N-N*], by region, 1985

trading bloc. The United States (USA) has relatively large endowments of its own resources but in order to support its large domestic final demand must import resources from abroad and is, as a result, a net consumer of global resources. While a proportion of this consumption is 'direct' a proportion is also accounted for by resources embodied in the produced goods that the USA imports. Japan (JPN) is the largest net consumer (in dollar terms) of any individual country. However, even though it has few resources of its own, this is offset to an extent because Japan exports produced goods to the rest of the world and, as discussed, these exports will have resources embodied in them: the 'indirect effect'. Canada is a slight surprise here as it is (marginally) a net consumer of global resources, although it is a large exporter of oil (in terms of value of its other resources) and metals. It should be noted, however, that Canada imports produced goods from the rest of the world particularly the USA and it is this indirect component of resource trade that is likely to be driving this finding.

The results in Figure 10.1 revealed that East Asia (EASIA) is, as a region, a net producer of global resources. Of course, this conclusion is an aggregate of different experiences across countries in this region. Hence, Figure 10.3 disaggregates [N-N*] across East Asia as follows. Net producers of resources include Indonesia (IDN), Malaysia (MYS) and China (CHN), primarily reflecting exports of oil and timber to the rest of the world. In contrast the 'tiger' economies – Taiwan (TAI), Singapore (SGP) and Hong Kong (HKG) – are net consumers of global resources. Clearly, the growth of domestic final demand in these small open economies has resulted in relatively large

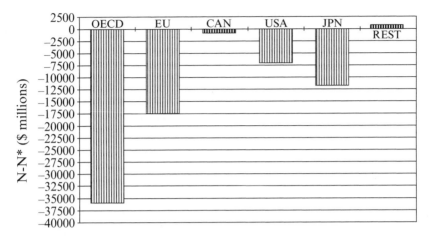

Figure 10.2   Net consumption of global resources [N-N], OECD, 1985*

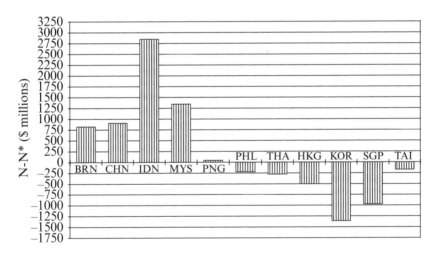

Figure 10.3   Net consumption of global resources [N-N], East Asia, 1985*

resource import requirements. Interestingly, both the Philippines (PHL) and Thailand (THA) are also net consumers of resources from the rest of the world.

Some important caveats to this empirical analysis need to be borne in mind, not least the relatively high degree of aggregation that we have used in our I/O model. Underlying this is an assumption that the value of resource depletion in a dollar of exports is equivalent to the value of resource depletion in a dollar of GNP. This will probably understate actual resource exports (and thereby imports to other countries). It is likely that a greater proportion of the exports of say, oil producers will be made up of resources. Secondly, it is also likely that traded produced goods (for example, heavy manufacturing) are more resource intensive than non-traded goods (for example, some light manufactures and services). Correcting these biases would impose greater data burdens on our Input/Output framework, necessitating at the very least identification of sectors such as primary production, services and manufacturing in each country.

It would also be interesting to examine the evolution of these linkages over time. The values of [N-N*] in 1980, 1985 and 1990 (all in 1985 constant prices) are illustrated in Figure 10.4. Clearly, variations in estimates of [N-N*] over time will depend on changes in the price (specifically the relevant rental rates) as well as changes in the quantity of resources traded. The OECD and Middle East and North Africa (MENA) dominate the overall picture. Figure 10.4 shows that in terms of the dollar value of [N-N*], consumption of global resources by the OECD decreased significantly in 1985 with little change in 1990 (relative to 1985). The mirror image of this is the experience of Middle East and North Africa. It is likely that these results reflect, to a large extent, changes in the international price of resources and in particular oil. World Bank (2000) indicates that the world price of oil in 1985 was 42 per cent lower than in 1980. Prices for several of the mineral resources covered in our data on resource depletion were also considerably lower in 1985 than in 1980. Hence, this general downward trend over the period between 1980 and 1985 is also exhibited (albeit less pronounced) in SSA and East Asia (EASIA). By contrast, a similar trend to that prevailing in the OECD is experienced in South Asia (SASIA) and Eastern Europe (EEUR).

The clear exception in Figure 10.4 is Latin America (LAM) where [N-N*] increased (but was slightly less in value in 1990 than in 1985). It may be that – even in the face of declining international resource prices – some of these countries have attempted to increase their exports of resources to the world to earn foreign exchange in order to service external debt. For example, World Bank data on the physical quantity of resource exports indicate that Mexico and Ecuador increased the quantity of oil exports by 51 per cent and 56 per cent from 1980–1990 respectively. Indeed, Figure 10.4 illustrates graphically that the analysis of linkages over time based only on the total value of resource flows is significantly affected by the (short-term) volatility of prices for certain resources. This suggests that it would also be interesting to extend our empirical model to analyse physical flows of traded resources as well as the total value of these flows.

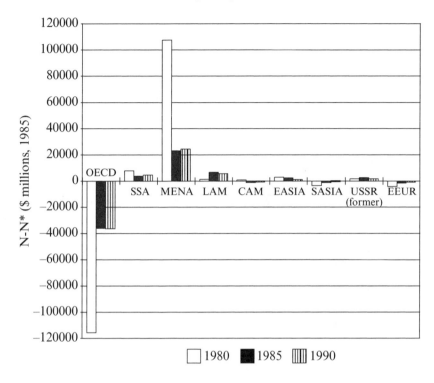

Figure 10.4   Net consumption of global resources [N-N*], 1980, 1985, 1990

Direct and Indirect Effects

The Input/Output framework used in this chapter measures *direct* trade in resources as well as *indirect* trade whereby resources are embodied in produced goods which are ultimately consumed elsewhere. To what extent is there a difference between empirical results using a narrow (but conventional) definition of resource trade based only on direct effects and a broader definition of resource trade based on both direct and indirect. In order to illustrate these magnitudes, we need to compare an ecological balance of payments when only resource flows to and from immediate trading partners have been taken into account with an ecological balance of payments when the country of final demand is taken account of.

In order to facilitate this comparison we need to identify those direct flows of resources. The simplest way to do this within our accounting framework is to assume that the share of resources in a country's total exports is equivalent to the share of resources in GNP (that is, n_i). We can then define a country's net *direct* consumption of global resources as

Wealth, welfare and sustainability

the sum of its (direct) resource exports minus its (direct) resource imports from other countries. This magnitude can then be compared to [N-N*], which measures net *indirect* consumption of global resources, as defined above. Figure 10.5 illustrates the difference between this narrow and broad definitions of resource trade for the year 1985 for trading blocs in the global economy (defined in Figure 10.1). It suggests that, in several cases, these differences are substantial.

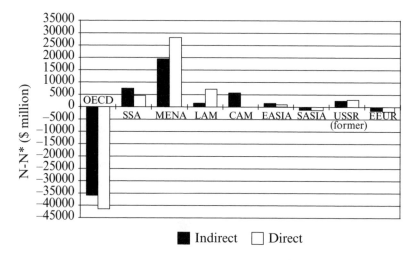

■ Indirect   □ Direct

Figure 10.5   Direct and indirect effects in selected regions

Firstly, net consumption of resources by the OECD bloc is larger when only direct effects are taken in account. This is readily explained in that this direct indicator does not take account of the subsequent use of those resources in the production of goods, which are exported to areas outside of the OECD.

Secondly, in the Middle Eastern and North African (MENA) region consideration of direct effects alone would indicate that this group of countries is a far larger net producer of resources than is the case where those resources embodied in imports to the region are brought into the reckoning. Similarly, the consideration of indirect effects substantially reduces the measured net production of resources of Latin America (LAM).

Thirdly, in Sub-Saharan Africa (SSA), East Asia (EASIA) and Central America (CAM), net consumption of global resources is relatively low when only direct effects are measured. To the extent that a country's imports of certain resources are subsequently embodied in the production of goods which are ultimately consumed elsewhere, this finding is one possible outcome. Indeed, Central America is a net consumer of resources for the direct effects only case but is a net producer of resources once indirect effects are also brought into the analysis.

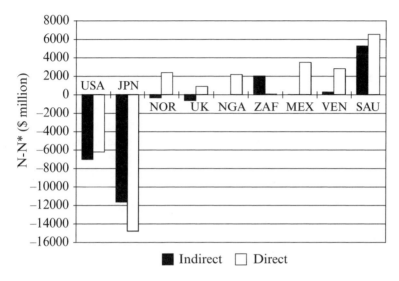

Figure 10.6   Direct and indirect effects in selected countries

The differences between these narrow (direct effects) and broader (direct and indirect effects) definitions of resource trade are illustrated for selected individual countries in Figure 10.6. This indicates that whereas the USA is a smaller net consumer of resources when only direct effects are taken into account, the opposite is true of Japan (JPN). Presumably, this can be explained largely by the embodiment of resources in produced goods imported to the USA and exported from Japan. In the case of the UK and Norway (NOR) it is notable that the position of apparent net producers of resources for the direct effects only case is transformed into a position of net consumption once indirect effects are also taken into account. For Venezuela (VEN), Mexico (MEX), Nigeria (NGA) and Saudi Arabia (SAU), the estimate of net production of resources is diminished once indirect effects are considered. However, for Saudi Arabia the relative magnitude between these narrow and broad measures of resource trade is less significant.

The Impact on Individual Countries

The above discussion described the extent to which a particular region or country relies on importing resources from the rest of the world to support its domestic final demand. It would also be interesting to identify those individual countries from which, for example, Japan's reliance on resource imports originates. This can be achieved by analysing in detail the elements of the total resource use matrix ($\mathbf{T}$):

$$\mathbf{T} = \mathbf{\hat{n}}'(\mathbf{I} - \mathbf{Q})^{-1}(\mathbf{c} \hat{+} \mathbf{i}) \qquad (10.9)$$

For example, the column sum in $\mathbf{T}$ denoting Japan describes the dollar value of resources that Japan uses to support its domestic final demand. The relevant individual elements of this column in turn constitute the dollar values of resources extracted in and exported from individual countries (in our sample) to Japan. Hence, while it is often asserted that Japan's domestic economy is heavily reliant on the imports of resources from Malaysia and Indonesia, our framework enables us to evaluate this claim in quantitative terms.

Table 10.4 provides a summary of estimates of imports from the main 10 countries upon whose resources, in dollar terms, the major trading blocs of Japan, the United States (USA) and the European Union (EU) were particularly reliant in 1985. The first column of data in the table gives the dollar value of Japan's (indirect) imports of resources from Indonesia. The second column of data also illustrates this magnitude as a percentage of the GNP of the exporter. Regarding the specific question of Japan's dependence on the resources of Indonesia and Malaysia, our estimates indicate that Japan imported resources valued at around $1474m from Indonesia, equivalent to 1.6 per cent of Indonesian GNP. For Malaysia, this magnitude is somewhat lower at $371m although this still corresponds to some 1.2 per cent of Malaysian GNP. While the degree to which Japan relies on imports from Indonesia and Malaysia is large, the absolute dollar value for Saudi Arabia and the United Arab Emirates is larger.

With respect to the experience of the USA, Table 10.4 indicates that this country imports resources across a range of countries. For Mexico and Venezuela the value of resource exports required to support the United States' domestic economy are $2423m and $1449m respectively. This is equivalent to 1.4 per cent and 2.2 per cent of GNP respectively for these countries. In Ecuador, the value of resource depletion that is required to support US domestic final demand is some 3.8 per cent of Ecuador's GNP. Canada and the United Kingdom are also identified as countries for which the dollar value of the USA's imported resource requirements is relatively high.

Finally, Table 10.4 identifies a number of African countries upon which EU countries rely for resources to support EU final demand. These are Algeria,

Table 10.4   *Resource dependency by country, 1985: Japan, USA, EU and*
              selected countries

Country	Resource imports ($m) (1)	As % of GNP of exporter (2)	Genuine savings (% of GNP) (3)
Japan – imports from:			
Brunei	509.5	13.4	–
China	312.2	0.1	13.7
Indonesia	1473.7	1.6	10.3
Kuwait	280.7	1.0	–19.2
Malaysia	371.1	1.2	14.5
Oman	999.0	10.7	–13.6
Qatar	675.2	9.8	–
Saudi Arabia	1854.9	1.9	–27.2
United Arab Emirates	2430.8	8.3	–5.9
United States	775.6	0.0	7.0
USA – imports from:			
Algeria	349.9	0.6	17.0
Canada	1380.4	0.4	11.2
Ecuador	412.6	3.8	–0.2
Indonesia	881.2	1.0	10.3
Mexico	2423.5	1.4	1.9
Nigeria	494.1	0.6	–23.9
Saudi Arabia	591.0	0.6	–27.2
United Arab Emirates	407.4	1.4	–5.9
United Kingdom	646.2	0.1	8.2
Venezuela	1448.7	2.2	–5.0
EU – imports from:			
Algeria	1152.9	2.0	17.0
Egypt, Arab Rep.	635.5	2.1	–0.6
Iraq	1314.5	3.4	–
Kuwait	864.0	3.2	–19.2
Libya	2611.7	10.1	–3.1
Nigeria	1298.3	1.6	–23.9
Norway	1464.4	2.4	11.6
Saudi Arabia	1398.7	1.4	–27.2
USSR (former)	1997.3	0.2	–
United States	1729.7	0.0	7.0

Sources: Authors' own estimates and World Bank (2001).

Egypt, Libya and Nigeria. Imports from the Middle Eastern countries of Saudi Arabia and Kuwait also appear to count for a large proportion of the EU's resource requirements. Similarly, the former USSR, USA and Norway also feature as substantial exporters of resources to the EU.

The final column in Table 10.4 provides an estimate of the period average genuine saving rate (1980 to 1990) in the resource-exporting countries that are reported here. The data are derived from World Bank (2000). Genuine savings are defined as gross savings net of asset consumption: that is, gross saving plus education expenditures (as an indicator of investment in human capital) minus the depreciation of produced capital and depletion of non-renewable and living resources.[4,5] These data are expressed in Table 10.4 as a percentage of GNP. It is interesting to note that of the (exporting) countries in the table for which data were available, nine countries had negative genuine savings over the period specified. In addition, the genuine savings rate in Mexico appears to be rather low. Half of the countries with which the USA has significant resource trade links have negative genuine saving (Ecuador, Nigeria, Saudi Arabia, United Arab Emirates and Venezuela). However, it is worth noting that none of the countries where genuine saving was negative are in the developed world. It also appears to be the case that Indonesia (upon which the USA and Japan are both relatively reliant for resources) and Malaysia (Japan only) did not exhibit negative genuine saving.

Negative genuine saving provides a signal of unsustainability in that it can be shown that, under certain circumstances, a point measure of negative genuine saving must lead to welfare declining along some interval in the future (Hamilton and Clemens, 1999). This leads naturally to a range of direct policy concerns in that a negative genuine savings rate, on this basis, implies that excessive consumption (whether by governments or households) has occurred for some reason. However, in practice, it appears that the prudent path of saving resource rents has been difficult to achieve for many countries (World Bank, 1997). One suggested reason for this might plausibly be the absence of effective institutions to reinvest productively the proceeds of resource depletion (Gelb and Associates, 1988; see also Chapter 5).

Drawing a link to our earlier discussion, this need not be interpreted as meaning that, for example, the USA is responsible for unsustainable behaviour in those countries (experiencing negative genuine saving) with which it trades. Rather, it is arguable that strong demand for the natural resources of an exporting country is only a proximate cause of unsustainable development, although some commentators have posited a more direct link between external indebtedness and resource exports (see, for an early but important discussion, Pearce et al., 1995). More generally, whether a country is on or off an unsustainable path will largely depend on whether its own policies are deficient and the ease of correcting this deficiency.

Nevertheless, it can be questioned as to whether resource importers will be entirely unconcerned about the sustainability prospects of their trading partners. This could be either because this could create risks for importers or because the long-term welfare of exporters is also a source of concern for importers. A tentative policy application of our framework is that, given this hypothesized concern, this analysis may provide the building blocks needed by importing countries if they wish to target assistance to exporting countries that are on an unsustainable path.

CONCLUSIONS

We have identified a number of reasons – both selfish and altruistic – why an 'ecological balance of payments' analysis may be of interest to, for example, policymakers in resource-importing countries. Using an Input/ Output framework, we have quantified the interdependencies that trade in natural resources gives rise to, by assessing the net consumption of global resources. This analysis takes account of direct and indirect trade in resources. Furthermore, we have disaggregated the implied resource imports of each country (the dollar value of global resources used to support a country's final demand) in order to identify those countries upon which Japan, the USA and the European Union are particularly reliant. Our analysis calculates in quantitative form what has been the subject of much speculation in qualitative form: that developed countries are reliant on developing countries for resources and that, furthermore, it can be claimed that many (but not all) of the latter are on an unsustainable path (that is, have negative genuine saving).

The observation of negative genuine savings is one example of the emerging evidence that many notable resource exporters have found the implementation of prudent resource and investment policies difficult to achieve. While resource importers are not responsible for the unsustainable behaviour of exporters, one implication of our analysis is that the latter may wish to assist, in some way, the former back onto a sustainable path. The link to our analysis of resource trade is that plausibly this assistance could come from those countries, which are particularly reliant on these exported resources. Of course, the extent to which this is a realistic proposition depends on the degree to which developed countries care about unsustainability in other countries.

A number of other extensions to our model suggest themselves. Firstly, changes in the value of resource flows over time are clearly significantly affected by the volatility of the prices of many of the resources that are commonly traded. It therefore would also be useful to examine changes in the volume of resources traded in addition to the value of these resources. Secondly, regarding the question of the conservation of living resources, it would be worthwhile to distinguish between living resources (for example, timber resources) and non-living resources (non-renewables) in future work.

NOTES

1. A distinct issue for the measurement of sustainability is how resource trade affects the terms of trade of importing and exporting countries (see, for example, Asheim, 1986 and Hartwick, 1994).
2. Strictly speaking, calculating [N-N*] requires that we rewrite N* (a row matrix) as N*' (a column matrix).
3. Now the Democratic Republic of Congo.
4. That is, oil, natural gas, coal, nickel, iron, bauxite, copper, zinc, lead, tin, phosphate, gold, silver and forest resources.
5. It should be noted that the theoretical frameworks underlying the measurement of genuine savings and our I/O analysis are somewhat different. That is, the latter assumes fixed coefficients whereas the former assumes substitution between relevant assets (or inputs).

11. Summary and conclusions

This book has dealt with what has been one of the fundamental questions in the sustainability debate: how can governments, most of whom have made a commitment to achieving sustainable development, know whether they are in fact on a sustainable path? Or, to state the problem slightly differently, how can current indicators tell us about future welfare? The theory we have expounded gives an unequivocal answer to the second question: the present value of utility will be increasing or decreasing along an optimal development path if genuine saving is positive or negative. If genuine saving is negative at a point on the optimal path, then this path is not sustainable.

The theory presented in this book concerns the properties of saving and the measurement of saving on the *optimal* development path for the economy. 'Real world' economies are not optimal, and often diverge substantially from optimality. Indeed, much of modern environmental and resource economics is premised on exactly this observation. Where does this leave the measurement of sustainability and future welfare?

One solution is offered by Dasgupta and Mäler (2000) who show that net saving has the same basic properties on non-optimal development paths if accounting prices are defined appropriately. However, this approach requires a forecast of future utility in order to define the accounting prices, in which case current saving indicators are not required in order to determine whether the economy is on a sustainable path.

The analysis and discussion in a number of chapters in this book can also be used to throw light on this crucial issue. For example, the empirical results on testing genuine saving in Chapter 4 were particularly useful with respect to the question of practical measures of sustainability. They suggested that saving, measured using shadow prices calculated in 'real-world' or non-optimal economies, is a reasonably strong predictor of future consumption (or the present value of changes in consumption, to be more precise). While the fit is (as we might expect) hardly perfect, practitioners can draw some comfort from the empirical analysis. Similarly, Chapter 5 showed that the combination of high resource dependence and negative genuine saving has been associated with lower growth in gross domestic product or GDP.

We also offered some more partial answers to the question of non-optimality. Chapter 7 argues that if there is excess deforestation, any decrease in this excess will result in higher measured saving *other things being equal* – that is, the economy will move in the direction of increasing social welfare. In other words, reducing excess deforestation will enhance development prospects. It is easy to see that a similar conclusion can be reached for efforts to decrease pollution in economies that exceed optimal pollution levels, where both the quantity of pollution and its shadow price will be higher than at the optimum (see, for example, Atkinson et al., 1997).

If we imagine an optimal economy with myopic policymakers, then Proposition 2.4 in Chapter 2 suggested that negative genuine saving can serve as an early warning of impending unsustainability because it will turn negative before the peak in utility on optimal paths with a single peak. As Hamilton and Hartwick (2005) show, this is precisely the case for the Dasgupta–Heal exhaustible resource economy.

Finally, Hamilton and Withagen (forthcomong) show that for competitive efficient economies, where firms maximize profits, households maximize utility and governments internalize externalities through Pigouvian taxes, there is in principle a general rule for sustainability: maintain positive genuine saving while ensuring that it grows at a rate less than the interest rate. They show that a particular instance of this rule, a fixed genuine saving rate, is feasible in the Dasgupta–Heal economy and leads to unbounded consumption.

We have covered a lot of ground in this book, and it is worth summarizing the highlights.

SUMMARY

Chapter 2 laid out the basic theoretical framework for what followed and, in doing so, offered four propositions on savings and wealth on optimal paths: (i) a development path with positive genuine saving will exhibit continuously increasing welfare; (ii) negative genuine saving at a point in time implies that future utility will be lower than current utility over some interval of time; (iii) if genuine saving is positive and grows at a rate less than the interest rate, then current utility and welfare both increase; and (iv) if a development path has a single peak, then genuine saving will turn negative before this peak is reached.

We then turned to the question of measuring genuine saving when there is a growing population. The figures published by the World Bank report total savings. If population is growing, then we need to account for the immiserating effects of this growth – existing assets will have to be shared with each new population cohort. The model developed in Chapter 3 showed that genuine saving should be measured as saving per person minus the product of the population growth rate and total wealth per capita. Estimates of total wealth (produced and natural) show wide variations in wealth composition and in wealth–output ratios across countries. Empirical estimates of genuine saving per person in 1999 showed that only six countries with high population growth rates (above 2 per cent per year) had increases in total wealth per capita, while 13 countries had a 'savings gap' (the increase in saving required to offset population growth) of over 20 per cent of gross national income or GNI.

The theory of genuine saving makes some very specific links between current saving and future utility or consumption. The fundamental result from Hamilton and Clemens (1999) is that current saving is equal to the (dollar value) change in the present value of future utility. This suggests that an empirical test of saving measures should be possible. Chapter 4 derived a formula equating genuine saving in the base year to the present value of changes in future consumption. This formula did not depend on the assumption of optimal growth, nor did it require restrictions such as constant returns to scale. The formula was tested econometrically for successive 20-year time intervals from 1976 to 1980, using four different measures of saving: gross, net, genuine and 'Malthusian' (factoring in population growth as described in Chapter 3). The savings tests showed that net saving is the worst 'predictor' of future change in consumption, with two of the five years exhibiting insignificant coefficients on saving and low explained variation. Malthusian saving explained the variation in the data well, but gives the worst fit with theory. The coefficient estimated suggested that the Malthusian adjustment overestimates the impact on future welfare. The savings gap mentioned above may therefore be overestimated, but even if the difference is a factor of two, the resultant saving gap would still be quite significant for most of the countries affected.

The analysis in Chapter 5 examined the extent to which resource-abundant countries have suffered a 'paradox of plenty' stemming from an inability to manage large resource revenues sustainably. Countries where economic performance has been poor are those where the combination of natural resource and public expenditure policies has led to a low rate of genuine saving. Chapter 6 followed on from this point in that it asked what if such countries actually had been prudent in the face of resource abundance? We looked at two investment rules. The first is where a country 'does just enough' to cover the depletion of natural resources. The second is where a country maintains genuine saving at a constant but modestly positive rate. Whether or not either rule is stringent is arguable. Regardless, the findings in this chapter indicated that many countries could be substantially richer if these rules had been followed. Using the proceeds of resource wealth to finance consumption now can have its justifications. This is a case to be argued. However, our analysis made clear that this comes at a likely future cost to development prospects.

Chapter 7 extended the savings analysis of earlier chapters to a domain that is both topical and important, the depletion of forests in the developing world. Central to this was an expansion of the asset boundary to account explicitly for changes in land use, that is, where land is an asset that has a distinct social value depending on the use to which it is put. In this way, an assessment could be made as to whether the switch of land use from forest to agriculture was actually wealth-increasing. Theory identifies a number of key parameters underlying this calculation in a precise manner. However, our empirical application with regards to how Peru might account for 'excess' deforestation suggests much more uncertainty about the magnitudes of these parameters in practice including local and global willingness to pay for conservation. Uncertainties also surround the question of whether there are thresholds: that is, 'minimum' areas of standing forest below which dramatic and adverse results for human welfare. Nevertheless, it is difficult to see how progress can be made in broadening the categories of natural assets covered by the savings analysis unless these and other measurement challenges are confronted.

Sustainable development is concerned with development prospects along a path stretching into the future. It is entirely plausible, and indeed to be expected, that technological change will intervene to alter the nature of this path. Indeed, much of modern growth theory has been predicated on the primacy of technological change in driving development. In Chapter 8 it was noted that some prominent contributions have presented the theory and illustrative calculations behind the claim that even a moderate but predictable flow of technological change might mean that productivity advances play the decisive role in determining prospects for sustainable development. Clearly, this issue merits serious consideration. However, the implications for measuring development prospects may be less dramatic than it at first appears if new knowledge creation is a costly process influenced by a variety of incentives.

Finally, chapters 9 and 10 have looked at two rather different aspects of the international dimension. The former provided an empirical assessment of how capital gains (or losses) earned on resources extracted in the future affect measures of sustainability. What this amounted to was a requirement that future resource price changes be reflected in current measures of genuine saving. Empirical results were presented for a large number of countries and a dozen resource commodities, using historical real price trends to forecast future prices. Reductions in saving in excess of 1 per cent of GNI were observed for over 20 countries, reflecting downward trends in the prices of the resources being depleted by these countries. Chapter 10 quantified inter-country (direct and indirect) flows of current natural resource rents in international trade. The onus, it was argued, is on resource-extracting countries to make provision for the loss of domestic natural assets whether for export or not. Yet, while from this perspective, these trade flows have no direct implications for measuring sustainability, it was interesting to note that a number of developed countries are highly dependent on resource depletion in developing countries which have experienced negative genuine saving rates. Such findings could form the basis of policies to assist exporters in adopting prudent resource and public investment policies.

FUTURE DIRECTIONS

It is more than 15 years since pioneering theoretical and empirical studies launched a new wave of interest in better accounting for social welfare. The distinguishing characteristic of this recent work is that it is not just concerned with greening the national accounts but also in measuring whether welfare is sustainable along a development path. That this field is going strong is both reassuring and an indication of the enormity of this research task that could scarcely have been envisaged a decade and a half ago. Recent contributions have not just sought to provide empirical extensions of established theory. A better understanding of the theoretical framework underlying the investigation of the properties of sustainability, and of its complexity and nuances, has also been a prominent feature of this work. Much progress has been made. Indeed, we hope that we have conveyed a lot of that progress in this book. However, there is still a lot to be learned and we take the opportunity in this last section to set out a few thoughts on future directions.

With regards to theory, we have already identified the important issue of social welfare and sustainability in non-optimal economies. More work on this topic is required. In addition, there is no shortage of empirical questions when it comes to measuring genuine saving. Among the challenges that appear the most urgent are the following:

- Inventorying and valuing the environmental services that underpin so much economic activity, whether it is pollination or regulation of flow in a watershed. While many of these values are captured indirectly in other asset values – the value of farmland, for example – the fact that there is no explicit valuation means that there are opportunities for unpleasant policy surprises.
- Valuing truly difficult assets such as biodiversity. This is a considerable challenge for those engaged in applying novel methods of valuation in

the field of environmental economics. Most studies to date typically have investigated the value that people place on (charismatic) individual species. Few studies to date value (changes in) habitat or diversity including, for example, non-use value. However, this work would be a crucial input in extending accounting approaches to this domain.

- Identifying non-linearities in the natural world that may not be captured in any simple way in measures of genuine saving. The implication that all is well because saving is positive may well be misleading if, subsequently, it is discovered that a major flip in natural systems has severe consequences for human welfare.
- Estimating elasticities of substitution for resources. The availability of databases of natural resource stocks and flows, in quantity and value terms, means that there should be more scope for exploring this important question – World Bank (2006: chapter 8) estimates the elasticity of substitution between land and fixed capital to be close to one, an important result. Despite its widely acknowledged importance, this issue has been the subject of surprisingly little investigation. Any further progress on accumulating evidence on this issue would be a valuable contribution indeed.

References

Aghion, P. and P. Howitt (1998), *Endogenous Growth Theory*, Cambridge, MA: MIT Press.

Aguirre, J. (1996), 'Environmental accounting: a practical application to the total valuation of the tropical rain forest', CATIE, Tarrialba, Costa Rica.

Ahmad, Y.J., S. El Serafy and E. Lutz (1989), *Environmental Accounting for Sustainable Development*, Washington DC: The World Bank.

Anielski, M. (1992), 'Accounting for carbon fixation by Alberta's forests and peatlands', paper presented at the Second Meeting of the International Society of Ecological Economists, Stockholm, August 3–6.

Aron, J. (1998), 'Political, economic and social institutions: review of growth evidence', WPS/98-4, Centre for the Study of African Economies, Institute of Economics and Statistics, University of Oxford.

Aronsson T., P.-O. Johansson, K.-G. Lofgren (1997), *Welfare Measurement, Sustainability and Green National Accounting*, Cheltenham, UK and Lyme, USA: Edward Elgar.

Arrow, K.J., P. Dasgupta and K.-G. Mäler (2003a), 'Evaluating projects and assessing sustainable development in imperfect economies', *Environmental and Resource Economics*, **26** (4), 647–85.

Arrow, K.J., P. Dasgupta and K.-G. Mäler (2003b), 'The genuine savings criterion and the value of population', *Economic Theory*, **21** (2–3), 217–25.

Arrow, K.J. et al. (2004), 'Are we consuming too much?', *Journal of Economic Perspectives*, **18** (3), 147–72.

Asheim, G.B. (1986), 'Hartwick's Rule in open economies', *Canadian Journal of Economics*, **86**, 395–402.

Asheim, G. and M. Weitzman (2001), 'Does NNP growth indicate welfare improvement?', *Economics Letters*, **73**, 233–9.

Asheim, G.B., W. Buchholz and C. Withagen (2003), 'The Hartwick Rule: myths and facts', *Environmental and Resource Economics*, **25**, 129–50.

Atkinson, G. and K. Hamilton (2003), 'Savings, growth and the resource curse hypothesis', *World Development*, **31** (11), 1771–92.

Atkinson, G., W.R. Dubourg, K. Hamilton, M. Munasinghe, D.W. Pearce and C.E.F. Young (1997), *Measuring Sustainable Development:*

Macroeconomics and Environment, Cheltenham, UK and Lyme, USA: Edward Elgar.

Auty, R. (ed.) (2001), *Resource Abundance and Economic Development*, WIDER Studies in Development Economics, Oxford: Oxford University Press.

Auty, R.M. and R.F. Mikesell (1998), *Sustainable Development in Mineral Economies*, Oxford: Clarendon Press.

Bailey, R.W. and R. Clarke (2000), 'Global macroeconomic sustainability: a dynamic general approach', *Environment and Development Economics*, **5**, 177–94.

Barbier, E.B. (1999), 'Endogenous growth and natural resource scarcity', *Environmental and Resource Economics*, **14**, 51–74.

Barro, R.J. and J.-W. Lee (1993), 'International comparisons of educational attainment', *Journal of Monetary Economics*, **32** (3), 363–94.

Barro, R. and X. Sala-i-Martin (1995), *Economic Growth*, New York: McGraw-Hill.

Bartelmus, P., E. Lutz and S. Schweinfest (1993), 'Integrated environmental and economic accounting: a case study for Papua New Guinea', in E. Lutz (ed.), *Toward Improved Accounting for the Environment*, Washington DC: World Bank.

Bosch, P. and B. Ensing (1996), 'Imports and the environment: sustainability costs of imported products', paper presented to the London Group, Stockholm.

Boscolo, M., J. Buongiorno and T. Panayotou (1997), 'Simulating options for carbon sequestration through improved management of a lowland tropical rainforest', *Environment and Development Economics*, **2**, 241–63.

British Petroleum (2001), *Statistical Review of World Energy*, London: BP plc.

Collins, S.M. and B.P. Bosworth (1996), 'Economic growth in East Asia: accumulation versus assimilation', *Brookings Papers on Economic Activity*, **2**, 135–203.

Corden, W.M. and J.P. Neary (1982), 'Booming sector and Dutch disease economics: a survey', *Economic Journal*, **92**, 826–44.

Dasgupta, P. (2000), 'Population and resources: an exploration of reproductive and environmental externalities', *Population and Development Review*, **26** (4), 643–89.

Dasgupta, P. (2001), *Human Well-being and the Natural Environment*, Oxford: Oxford University Press.

Dasgupta, P. and G. Heal (1979), *Economic Theory and Exhaustible Resources*, Cambridge: Cambridge University Press.

Dasgupta, P. and K.-G. Mäler (2000), 'Net national product, wealth, and social well-being', *Environment and Development Economics*, **5**, Parts 1 and 2, 69–93, February and May 2000.

Davis, G. (1995), 'Learning to love the Dutch disease', *World Development*, **23** (10), 1765–79.

Dixit, A., P. Hammond and M. Hoel (1980), 'On Hartwick's Rule for regular maximin paths of capital accumulation and resource depletion', *Review of Economic Studies*, **XLVII**, 551–6.

Ekins, P., C. Folke, R. Groot, S. de Simon, L. Deutsch, J. Perk, A. van de Chiesura, A. Vliet, K. van Skanberg, J.M. Douguet and M. O'Connor (2003), 'Identifying critical natural capital', *Ecological Economics*, **44** (2–3), 159–292.

Fankhauser, S. (1994), 'Evaluating the social costs of greenhouse gas emissions', *Energy Journal*, **15** (2), 157–84.

Fankhauser, S., R.S.J. Tol and D.W. Pearce (1997), 'The aggregation of climate change damages: a welfare theoretic approach', *Environment and Resource Economics*, **10** (3), 249–66.

Felipe, J. (1999), 'Total factor productivity growth in East Asia: a critical survey', *Journal of Development Studies*, **35** (4), 1–41.

Ferreira, S. and J.R. Vincent (2005), 'Genuine savings: leading indicator of sustainable development?', *Economic Development and Cultural Change*, **53**, 737–54.

Ferreira, S., K. Hamilton and J. Vincent (2003), 'Comprehensive wealth and future consumption', mimeo, Washington: The World Bank.

FIL (Forestal International Limited) (1975), *Inventario Forestal del Bosque Nacional Alejandro von Humboldt, Región de Pucallpa, Perú*, Food and Agricultural Organization, FAO, Rome.

Førsund, F.R. (1985), 'Input-Output models, national economic models and the environment', in A.V. Kneese and J.L. Sweeney (eds), *Handbook of Natural Resource and Energy Economics*, Amsterdam: North-Holland.

Gates, J.H. (1984), 'Human capital investment in health: a measurement framework and estimates for the United States 1952–78', *Review of Income and Wealth*, **30** (1), 39–52.

Gelb, A., Associates (1988), *Oil Windfalls: Blessing or Curse?*, Oxford: Oxford University Press.

Groom, B., C. Hepburn, P. Koundouri and D.W. Pearce (2005), 'Discounting the future: the long and the short of it', *Environmental and Resource Economics*, **32** (4), 445–94.

Grossman, M. (1972), 'On the concept of health capital and the demand for health', *Journal of Political Economy*, **80**, 223–55.

Gylfason, T. (2001), 'Natural resources, education and development', *European Economic Review*, **45**, 847–59.

Hamilton, K. (1995), 'GNP and genuine savings', Centre for Social and Economic Research on the Global Environment (CSERGE), University College London and University of East Anglia.

Hamilton, K. (1997), 'Forest resources and national income', Environment Department, The World Bank, Washington.

Hamilton, K. (2000), 'Sustaining economic welfare: estimating changes in wealth per capita', Policy Research Working Paper 2498, November, The World Bank, Washington DC.

Hamilton, K. (2002), 'Sustaining per capita welfare with growing population: theory and measurement', Environment Department, The World Bank, Washington DC.

Hamilton, K. (2003), 'Sustaining economic welfare: estimating changes in total and per capita wealth', *Environment, Development and Sustainability*, **5**, 419–36.

Hamilton, K. and K. Bolt (2004), 'Resource price trends and development prospects', *Portuguese Economic Journal*, Special Issue on Environmental Economics, **3**, 85–97.

Hamilton, K. and M. Clemens (1999), 'Genuine saving in developing countries', *World Bank Economic Review*, **13** (2), 333–56.

Hamilton, K. and J.M. Hartwick (2005), 'Investing exhaustible resource rents and the path of consumption', *Canadian Journal of Economics*, **38** (2), 615–21.

Hamilton, K. and C. Withagen (forthcoming), 'Savings, welfare and rules for sustainability', *Canadian Journal of Economics*.

Hamilton, K., G. Atkinson and D.W. Pearce (1998), 'Sustainability and savings rules: selected extensions', Centre for Social and Economic Research on the Global Environment (CSERGE), University College London and University of East Anglia.

Hamilton, K., G. Ruta and L. Tajibaeva (2005), 'Capital accumulation and resource depletion: a Hartwick Rule counterfactual', Policy Research Working Paper 3480, January, The World Bank, Washington DC.

Haripriya, G.S. (2000), 'Integrating forest resources into the system of national accounts in Maharashtra', *Environment and Development Economics*, **5**, 143–56.

Haripriya, G.S. (2003), 'Carbon budget of the Indian forest ecosystem', *Climatic Change*, **56** (3), 291–319.

Hartwick, J.M. (1977), 'Intergenerational equity and the investing of rents from exhaustible resources', *American Economic Review*, **66**, 972–74.

Hartwick, J.M. (1990), 'Natural resources, national accounting and economic depreciation', *Journal of Public Economics*, **43**, 291–304.

Hartwick, J.M. (1992), 'Deforestation and national accounting', *Environmental and Resource Economics*, **2**, 513–21.

Hartwick, J.M. (1993), 'Forestry economics, deforestation and national accounting', in E. Lutz (ed.), *Toward Improved Accounting for the Environment*, Washington DC: The World Bank.

Hartwick, J.M. (1994), 'Constant consumption paths in open economies with exhaustible resources', *Review of International Economics*, **31** (3), 275–83.

Hassan, R.M. (2000), 'Improved measure of the contribution of cultivated forests to national income and wealth in South Africa', *Environment and Development Economics*, **5**, 157–76.

Hoffrén, J. (1996), 'Measuring the ecological quality of Finnish forest resources', Research Report No. 220, Statistics Finland, Helsinki.

Hultkrantz, L. (1992), 'National account of timber and forest environmental resources in Sweden', *Environmental and Resource Economics*, **2**, 283–305.

IMF (International Monetary Fund) (various years), *Direction of Trade Statistics Yearbook*, Washington DC: International Monetary Fund.

International Energy Agency (1995), *Coal Information 1994*, Paris: OECD.

International Energy Agency (2001), *Coal Information 2001*, Paris: OECD.

Jones, C.I. (1998), *Introduction to Economic Growth*, New York: W.W. Norton & Company.

Jorgenson, D.W. (1995), *Productivity*, Cambridge, MA: MIT Press.

Katila, M. (1995), 'Accounting for market and non-market production of timber, fuelwood and fodder in the national income accounting framework: a case study', *Banko Janakari*, **5** (1), 18–25.

Klepper, G. and F. Stähler (1998), 'Sustainability in closed and open economies', *Review of International Economics*, **63**, 488–506.

Kramer, R.A. and D.E. Mercer (1997), 'Valuing a global environmental good: US residents' willingness to pay to protect tropical rain forests', *Land Economics*, **73** (2), 196–210.

Kunte, A., K. Hamilton, J. Dixon and M. Clemens (1998), 'Estimating national wealth: methodology and results', Environment Department Papers, Environmental Economics Series, Paper No. 57. The World Bank, Washington DC.

Lampietti, J. and J. Dixon (1995), *To See the Forest for the Trees: A Guide to Non-Timber Forest Benefits*, Environment Department, Washington DC: The World Bank.

Lane, P.R. and A. Tornell (1996), 'Power, growth and the voracity effect', *Journal of Economic Growth*, **1**, 213–41.

Lange, G.-M. and M. Wright (2004), 'Sustainable development in mineral economies: the example of Botswana', *Environment and Development Economics*, **9** (4), 485–505.

Lind, R.C. and R.E. Schuller (1998), 'Equity and discounting in climate change decisions', in W.D. Nordhaus (ed.), *Economics and Policy Issues in Climate Change*, Resources for the Future, Washington DC: The World Bank.

Link, P.M. and R.S.J. Tol (2004), 'Possible economic impacts of a shutdown of the thermohaline circulation: an application of fund', *Portuguese Economic Journal*, Special Issue on Environmental Economics, **3** (2), 99–114.

Mäler, K.-G. (1991), 'National accounts and environmental resources', *Environmental and Resource Economics*, **1**, 1–15.

Mankiw, N.G., D. Romer and D.N. Weil (1992), 'A contribution to the empirics of economic growth', *Quarterly Journal of Economics*, **107** (2), 407–37.

Martinez-Alier, J. (1995), 'The environment as a luxury good or "too poor to be green"', *Ecological Economics*, **13**, 1–10.

Matsuyama, K. (1992), 'Agricultural productivity, comparative advantage and economic growth', *Journal of Economic Theory*, **58**, 317–34.

McMahon, G. (1997), *The Natural Resource Curse: Myth or Reality?*, Washington DC: World Bank Economic Development Institute.

Miller, R.E. and P.D. Blair (1985), *Input-Output Analysis: Foundations and Extensions*, Englewood Cliffs, NJ: Prentice-Hall,

Mourato, S. and J. Smith (2002), 'Can carbon trading reduce deforestation by slash-and-burn farmers? Evidence from the Peruvian Amazon', in D.W. Pearce, C. Pearce and C. Palmer (eds), *Valuing the Environment in Developing Countries*, Cheltenham, UK and Northampton, MA, USA: Edward Elgar.

Nalvarte, W. (1999), 'Estimando el valor de la deforestacion en El Peru', report to the Environment Department, The World Bank, Washington DC.

Nordhaus, W.D. (1995), 'How should we measure sustainable income?', mimeo, Yale University.

Nordhaus, W.D. and E.C. Kokkelenberg (eds) (1999), *Nature's Numbers: Expanding the National Economic Accounts to Include the Environment*, Washington DC: National Academy Press.

OAS (Organisation of American States)/UNEP (United Nations Environment Programme)/Government of Peru (1987), *Minimum Conflict: Guidelines for Planning the Use of American Humid Tropic Environments*, Washington DC: OAS.

OECD (1994), 'Foreign Trade Statistics by Commodity: Series C', Paris: Organisation for Economic Cooperation and Development.

Pearce, D.W. (2003), 'The social cost of carbon and its policy implications', *Oxford Review of Economic Policy*, **19**, 362–84.

Pearce, D.W. and G. Atkinson (1993), 'Capital theory and the measurement of sustainable development: an indicator of weak sustainability', *Ecological Economics*, **8**, 103–8.

Pearce, D.W. and D. Ulph (1999), 'A social discount rate for the United Kingdom', in D.W. Pearce (ed.), *Economics and Environment: Essays on Ecological Economics and Sustainable Development*, Cheltenham, UK and Northampton, MA, USA: Edward Elgar.

Pearce, D.W., W.N. Adger, D. Maddison and D. Moran (1995), 'Debt and the environment', *Scientific American*, June, 28–32.

Pearce, D.W., A. Markandya and E.B. Barbier (1989), *Blueprint for a Green Economy*, London: Earthscan.

Pearce, D.W., F. Putz and J.K. Vanclay (1999), 'A sustainable forest future?', Natural Resources International, UK and UK Department for International Development, London.

Pedersen, O.G. (1993), 'Input–output analysis and emissions of CO_2, SO_2 and NO_X: the linkage of physical and monetary data', paper presented to the Tenth International Conference on Input-Output Techniques, Seville.

Pemberton, M. and D. Ulph (2001), 'Measuring income and measuring sustainability', *Scandinavian Journal of Economics*, **103** (1), 25–40.

Peskin, H.M. (1989), 'Accounting for natural resource depletion and degradation in developing countries', Environment Department Working Paper No. 13, The World Bank, Washington DC.

Pezzey, J.C.V. (1989), 'Economic analysis of sustainable growth and sustainable development', Environment Department Working Paper No. 15, The World Bank, Washington DC.

Pezzey, J.C.V. (1997), 'Sustainability constraints versus "optimality" versus intertemporal concern and axioms versus data', *Land Economics*, **73**, 448–66.

Pezzey, J.C.V., N. Hanley, K. Turner and D. Tinch (forthcoming), 'Comparing augmented sustainability measures for Scotland: is there a mismatch?', *Ecological Economics*, in press.

Pritchett, L. (1996), 'Where has all the education gone?', Policy Research Working Paper 1581, The World Bank, Washington DC.

Pritchett, L. (2000), 'The tyranny of concepts: CUDIE (cumulated, depreciated, investment effort) is *not* capital', *Journal of Economic Growth*, **5** (December), 361–84.

Proops, J.L.R. and G. Atkinson (1998), 'A practical sustainability criterion when there is international trade', in S. Faucheux, M. O'Connor and J. van den Straaten (eds), *Sustainable Development: Analysis and Public Policy*, Dordrecht: Kluwer Academic Publishers.

Proops, J.L.R., G. Atkinson, B.F. von Schlotheim and S. Simon (1999), 'International trade and the sustainability footprint: a practical criterion for its assessment', *Ecological Economics*, **28**, 75–97.

Rees, W.E. and M. Wackernagel (1994), 'Appropriated carrying capacity: measuring the natural capital requirements of the human economy', in A.M. Jansson, M. Hammer, C. Folke and R. Costanza (eds), *Investing in Natural Capital: The Ecological Economics Approach to Sustainability*, Washington DC: Island Press.

Repetto, R., W. Magrath, M. Wells, C. Beer and F. Rossini (1989), *Wasting Assets: Natural Resources in the National Accounts*, Washington DC: World Resources Institute.

Rivera, C. (1985), *Volúmenes de Madera Extraídos en las Parcelas de la Colonización Forestal Von Humboldt*, Empresa Agroforestal Von Humboldt S.A. Promotor Proyecto Especial Pichis, Palcazú Sp.

Sachs, J.D. and A.M. Warner (1995), 'Natural resource abundance and economic growth', Development Discussion Paper No. 517, Harvard Institute of International Development, Cambridge, Mass.

Sachs, J.D. and A.M. Warner (1997), 'Sources of slow growth in African economies', *Journal of African Economies*, **6** (3), 335–76.

Sachs, J.D. and A.M. Warner (1999), 'Natural resource intensity and economic growth', in J. Mayer, B. Chambers and A. Farooq (eds), *Development Policies in Natural Resource Economies*, Cheltenham, UK and Northampton, MA, USA: Edward Elgar.

Sachs, J.D. and A.M. Warner (2001), 'The curse of natural resources', *European Economic Review*, **45**, 827–38.

Sala-i-Martin, X. (1997), 'I just ran two million regressions', *American Economic Review*, **87** (2), 178–83.

Sarraf, M. and M. Jiwanji (2001), 'Beating the resource curse: the case of Botswana', Environment Department Working Papers, Environmental Economics Series No. 83, The World Bank, Washington DC.

Scarpa, R., J. Buongiorno, J.S. Hseu and K. Lee (2000), 'Assessing the non-timber value of forests: a revealed preference, hedonic model of Wisconsin hardwoods', *Journal of Forest Economics*, **6** (2), 83–107.

Schneider, R. (1995), 'Government and the economy on the Amazon frontier', Environment Paper No. 11, The World Bank, Washington DC.

Seroa da Motta, R. and C.A. Ferraz (2000), 'Estimating timber depreciation in the Brazilian Amazon', *Environment and Development Economics*, **5**, 129–42.

Solórzano, R., R. de Camino, R. Woodward, J. Tosi, V. Watson, A. Vásquez, C. Villalobos, J. Jiménez, R. Repetto and W. Cruz (1991), *Accounts*

Overdue: Natural Resource Depreciation in Costa Rica, Washington DC: World Resources Institute.

Solow, R. (1986), 'On the intergenerational allocation of natural resources', *Scandinavian Journal of Economics*, **88** (1), 141–9.

Stijns, J.-P.C. (2000), 'Natural resource abundance and economic growth revisited', mimeo, University of California at Berkeley.

Takayama, A. (1980), 'Optimal technical progress with exhaustible resources', in M.C. Kemp and N.V. Long (eds), *Exhaustible Resources, Optimality and Trade*, Amsterdam: North Holland.

Temple, J. (1999), 'The new growth evidence', *Journal of Economic Literature*, **XXXVII**, 112–56.

Tol, R.S.J. (2003), 'The marginal costs of carbon dioxide emissions: an assessment of the uncertainties', Research Unit on Sustainability and Global Change FNU-19, Centre for Marine and Climate Research, Hamburg University, Hamburg.

Tol, R., T. Downing, S. Fankhauser, R. Richels and J. Smith (2001), 'Progress in estimating the marginal costs of greenhouse gas emissions', *Pollution Atmosphérique*, December, 155–79.

Torres, M. (2000), 'The total economic value of Amazonian deforestation, 1978–1993', *Ecological Economics*, **33**, 283–97.

United Nations (1993), *System of National Accounts*, ST/ESA/STAT/SER. F/2/Rev.4., New York: United Nations.

United Nations Conference on Trade and Development (UNCTAD) (2001), *Monthly Commodity Price Bulletin*, Vol. LV No. 7 July 2001, New York.

US Geological Survey (2001a), *Minerals Yearbook*, Washington DC, http://minerals.usgs.gov/minerals/pubs/myb.html.

US Geological Survey (2001b), *Mineral Commodity Summaries*, Washington DC, http://minerals.usgs.gov/minerals/pubs/mcs/.

van Kooten, G.C. and E. Bulte (2000), *The Economics of Nature: Managing Biological Assets*, Oxford: Blackwell.

van Kooten, G.C., R.A. Sedjo and E.H. Bulte (1999), 'Tropical deforestation: issues and policies', in H. Folmer and T. Tietenberg (eds), *International Yearbook of Environmental and Resource Economics 1999/2000*, Cheltenham, UK and Northampton, MA, USA: Edward Elgar.

van Tongeren, J., S. Schweinfest, E. Lutz, M. Gomez Luna and G. Martin (1993), 'Integrated environmental and economic accounting: a case study for Mexico', in E. Lutz (ed.), *Toward Improved Accounting for the Environment*, Washington DC: The World Bank.

Vincent, J.R. (1997), 'Resource depletion and economic sustainability in Malaysia', *Environmental and Development Economics*, **2**, 19–37.

Vincent, J.R. (1999a), 'A framework for forest accounting', *Forest Science*, **45** (4), 1–10.

Vincent, J.R. (1999b), 'Net accumulation of timber resources', *Review of Income and Wealth*, **45** (2), 251–62.

Vincent, J.R. and J.M. Hartwick (1997), *Accounting for the Benefits of Forest Resources: Concepts and Experience*, FAO Forestry Department, Rome: Food and Agriculture Organisation.

Vincent, J., T. Panayotou, and J.M. Hartwick (1997), 'Resource depletion and sustainability in small open economies', *Journal of Environmental Economics and Management*, **33**, 274–86.

Vincent, J.R., L.F. Wan, Y.T. Chang, M. Noriha and G.W.H. Davison (1993), *Malaysian National Conservation Strategy. Volume 4: Natural Resource Accounting*, Economic Planning Unit, Prime Minister's Department, Kuala Lumpur.

Wackernagel, M., L. Onisto, P. Bello, A. Linares, I. Falfan, J. Garcia, A. Guerrero and G. Guerrero (2000), 'Natural capital accounting with the ecological footprint concept', *Ecological Economics*, **29**, 375–90.

Weitzman, M.L. (1976), 'On the welfare significance of national product in a dynamic economy', *Quarterly Journal of Economics*, **90** (1), 156–62.

Weitzman, M.L. (1997), 'Sustainability and technical progress', *Scandinavian Journal of Economics*, **99** (1), 1–13.

Weitzman, M.L. and K.G. Löfgren (1997), 'On the welfare significance of green accounting as taught by parable', *Journal of Environmental Economics and Management*, **32**, 139–53.

World Bank (1997), *Expanding the Measure of Wealth: Indicators of Sustainable Development*, ESD Studies and Monographs Series No. 17, Washington DC: The World Bank.

World Bank (1999), *World Development Indicators 1999*, Washington DC: The World Bank.

World Bank (2000), *World Development Indicators 2000*, Washington DC: The World Bank.

World Bank (2001), *World Development Indicators 2001*, Washington DC: The World Bank.

World Bank (2002a), *World Development Indicators 2002*, Washington DC: The World Bank.

World Bank (2002b), 'Manual for calculating adjusted net savings', mimeo, The World Bank, Washington DC, http://www.worldbank.org/environmentaleconomics.

World Bank (2003), *World Development Indicators 2003*, Washington DC: The World Bank.

World Bank (2004), *World Development Indicators 2004*, Washington DC: The World Bank.

World Bank (2006), *Where is the Wealth of Nations?*, Washington DC: The World Bank.

World Resources Institute (1998), *World Resources 1998–1999*, Washington DC: World Resources Institute.

Young, A. (1994), 'Lessons from the East Asian NICs: a contrarian view', *European Economic Review*, **38**, 964–73.

Young, A. (1995), 'The tyranny of numbers: confronting the statistical realities of the East Asian growth experience', *Quarterly Journal of Economics*, **110**, 641–80.

Young, C.E.F. (1996), 'Economic adjustment policies and the environment: a case study of Brazil', unpublished PhD thesis, University College London.

Zerbe, R. and D. Dively (1994), *Benefit–cost Analysis in Theory and Practice*, New York: Harper Collins College Publishers.

Index

absorptive capacity 83
accounting prices 6–7, 173
acid rain 155
Africa, *see* Middle East and North
    Africa; Sub-Saharan Africa
Aghion, P. 125, 128
agricultural land, conversion of forest
    land into, *see* deforestation
agricultural productivity 105–8
agricultural sector, economic
    performance of 56
agriculture, forestry and fisheries, asset
    value of 18, 19, 20, 41
Aguirre, J. 93
Ahmad, Y.J. 1
aid inflows 23, 154
Algeria 34, 55, 79, 81, 88, 149, 168,
    169
altruism 154
Angola 146
Anielski, M. 93
Argentina
    composition of wealth in 20
    genuine saving in 24, 148
    investment in 80, 82, 89
    wealth per capita in 34
        change in 25, 34
Armenia 149
Aron, J. 57
Aronsson, T. 6
Arrow, K.J. 6, 7
Asheim, G.B. 5, 38, 83, 172
Asia, *see* East Asia; Eastern Europe
    and Central Asia; South Asia
asset to GDP ratio 18
Atkinson, G. 2, 5, 6, 70, 153, 155, 159,
    174
Australia 34, 145, 146, 148, 151
Austria 34, 149
Auty, R.M. 54
average harvesting costs 101

Bailey, R.W. 153, 155
Bangladesh 26, 31, 34, 55, 90
Barbier, E.B. 70
Barro, R.J. 57, 60, 70, 118, 121
Bartelmus, P. 93
bauxite 18, 57, 77, 80, 143, 151, 161
Belarus 149
Belgium 34, 90
Benin 34, 89
biodiversity 93, 116, 177–8
Blair, P.D. 155
Bolivia
    composition of wealth in 20
    genuine saving in 23, 24, 149
    investment in 79, 88
    wealth per capita in 34
        change in 23, 25, 34
Bolt, K. 147
Bosch, P. 154
Boscolo, M. 102
Bosnia and Herzegovina 150
Bosworth, B.P. 121, 122, 129–30, 135,
    136
Botswana 73, 83, 146, 148
Brazil
    composition of wealth in 20
    genuine saving in 24, 148
    investment in 78, 79, 89
    market share of resources 151
    pollution in 155
    resource depletion and gross saving
        in 55
    returns from pasture in 108
    wealth per capita in 34
        change in 25, 34
British Petroleum 143
Brunei 163, 169
Bulgaria 148
Bulte, E. 155
Burkina Faso 34
Burundi 34, 90, 149